Trevor Baker

# ESSENTIALS

## OCR Twenty First Century
## GCSE Physics A
### Revision Guide

# Ideas about Science

The OCR Twenty First Century Physics specification aims to ensure that you develop **an understanding of science itself** – of how scientific knowledge is obtained, the kinds of evidence and reasoning behind it, its strengths and limitations, and how far we can rely on it.

These issues are explored through Ideas about Science, which are built into the specification content and summarised over the following pages.

The tables below give an overview of the Ideas about Science that can be assessed in each unit and provide examples of content which support them in this guide.

## Unit A181 (Modules P1, P2 and P3)

| Ideas about Science | Example of Supporting Content |
|---|---|
| Cause–effect explanations | Cell Damage (page 17) |
| Developing scientific explanations | The Solar System (page 10) |
| The scientific community | Continental Drift (page 5) |
| Risk | Choosing Energy Sources (page 32) |
| Making decisions about science and technology | Choosing Energy Sources (page 32) |

## Unit A182 (Modules P4, P5 and P6)

| Ideas about Science | Example of Supporting Content |
|---|---|
| Data: their importance and limitations | Measuring the Half-life (page 60) |
| Cause–effect explanations | Background Radiation (page 59) |
| Developing scientific explanations | Alpha Particle Scattering Experiment (page 64) |
| Risk | Uses of Radiation (page 61) |
| Making decisions about science and technology | Nuclear Waste (page 62) |

## Unit A183 (Module P7)

| Ideas about Science | Example of Supporting Content |
|---|---|
| Data: their importance and limitations | The Hubble Constant (page 78) |
| Cause–effect explanations | Absolute Zero (page 80) |
| Developing scientific explanations | Using a Star's Spectrum (page 81) |
| The scientific community | The Curtis–Shapley Debate (page 77) |
| Risk | Solar and Lunar Eclipses (page 71) |
| Making decisions about science and technology | Funding Developments in Science (page 85) |

## Data: Their Importance and Limitations

Science is built on **data**. Physicists carry out experiments to collect and interpret data, seeing whether the data agree with their explanations. If the data do agree, then it means the current explanation is more likely to be correct. If not, then the explanation has to be changed.

Experiments aim to find out what the '**true**' value of a quantity is. Quantities are affected by **errors** made when carrying out the experiment and **random variation**. This means that the measured value may be different to the true value. Physicists try to **control** all the factors that could cause this uncertainty.

Physicists always take **repeat readings** to try to make sure that they have accurately estimated the true value of a quantity. The **mean** is calculated and is the best estimate of what the true value of a quantity is. The more times an experiment is repeated, the greater the chance that a result near to the true value will fall within the mean.

The **range**, or spread, of data gives an indication of where the true value must lie. Sometimes a measurement will not be in the zone where the majority of readings fall. It may look like the result (called an '**outlier**') is wrong – however, it doesn't automatically mean that it is. The outlier has to be checked by repeating the measurement of that quantity. If the result can't be checked, then it should still be used.

Here is an example of an outlier in a set of data:

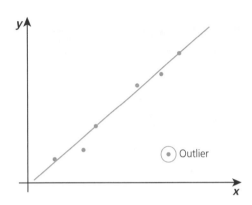

HT The spread of the data around the mean (the range) gives an idea of whether it really is different to the mean from another measurement. If the ranges for each mean don't overlap, then it's more likely that the two means are different. However, sometimes the ranges do overlap and there may be no significant difference between them.

The ranges also give an indication of **reliability** – a wide range makes it more difficult to say with certainty that the true value of a quantity has been measured. A small range suggests that the mean is closer to the true value.

If an outlier is discovered, you need to be able to defend your decision as to whether you keep it or discard it.

# Ideas about Science

## Cause–Effect Explanations

Science is based on the idea that a **factor** has an **effect** on an outcome. Physicists make predictions as to how the **input variable** will change the **outcome variable**. To make sure that only the input variable can affect the outcome, physicists try to control all the other variables that could potentially alter it. This is called '**fair testing**'.

You need to be able to explain why it's necessary to control all the factors that might affect the outcome. This means suggesting how they could influence the outcome of the experiment.

A **correlation** is where there's an apparent link between a factor and an outcome. It may be that as the factor increases, the outcome increases as well. On the other hand, it may be that when the factor increases, the outcome decreases.

For example, in a wire of constant cross-sectional area at constant temperature, there's a correlation that the longer the wire, the more resistance it has.

Just because there's a correlation doesn't necessarily mean that the factor causes the outcome. Further experiments are needed to establish this. It could be that another factor causes the outcome or that both the original factor and outcome are caused by something else.

The following graph suggests a correlation between going to the opera regularly and living longer. It's far more likely that if you have the money to go to the opera, you can afford a better diet and health care. Going to the opera isn't the true cause of the correlation.

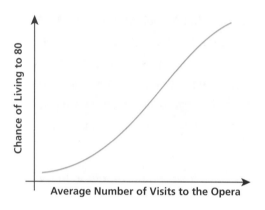

Sometimes the factor may alter the chance of an outcome occurring but doesn't guarantee it will lead to it. The statement 'the more time spent on a sun bed the greater the chance of developing skin cancer' is an example of this type of correlation, as some people will not develop skin cancer even if they do spend a lot of time on a sun bed.

To investigate claims that a factor increases the chance of an outcome, physicists have to study groups of people who either share as many factors as possible or are chosen randomly to try to ensure that all factors will present in people in the test group. The larger the experimental group, the more confident physicists can be about the conclusions made.

(HT) Even so, a correlation and cause will still not be accepted by physicists unless there's a scientific mechanism that can explain them.

# Ideas about Science

## Developing Scientific Explanations

Physicists devise **hypotheses** (predictions of what will happen in an experiment), along with an **explanation** (the scientific mechanism behind the hypotheses) and **theories** (that can be tested).

Explanations involve thinking creatively to work out why data have a particular pattern. Good scientific explanations account for most or all of the data already known. Sometimes they may explain a range of phenomena that weren't previously thought to be linked. Explanations should enable predictions to be made about new situations or examples.

When deciding on which is the better of two explanations, you should be able to give reasons why.

Explanations are tested by comparing predictions based on them with data from observations or experiments. If there's an agreement between the experimental findings, then it increases the chance of the explanation being right. However, it doesn't prove it's correct. Likewise, if the prediction and observation indicate that one or the other is wrong, it decreases the confidence in the explanation on which the prediction is based.

## The Scientific Community

Once a physicist has carried out enough experiments to back up his/her claims, they have to be reported. This enables the **scientific community** to carefully check the claims, something which is required before they're accepted as scientific knowledge.

Physicists attend **conferences** where they share their findings and sound out new ideas and explanations. This can lead to physicists revisiting their work or developing links with other laboratories to improve it.

The next step is writing a formal **scientific paper** and submitting it to a **journal** in the relevant field. The paper is allocated to **peer reviewers** (experts in their field), who carefully check and evaluate the paper. If the peer reviewers accept the paper, then it's published. Physicists then read the paper and check the work themselves.

New scientific claims that haven't been evaluated by the whole scientific community have less credibility than well-established claims.

It takes time for other physicists to gather enough evidence that a theory is sound. If the results can't be **repeated** or **replicated** by themselves or others, then physicists will be sceptical about the new claims.

If the explanations can't be arrived at from the available data, then it's fair and reasonable for different physicists to come up with alternative explanations. These will be based on the background and experience of the physicists. It's through further experimentation that the best explanation will be chosen.

This means that the current explanation has the greatest support. New data aren't enough to topple it. Only when the new data are sufficiently repeated and checked will the original explanation be changed.

(HT) You need to be able to suggest reasons why an accepted explanation will not be given up immediately when new data, which appear to conflict with it, have been published.

# Ideas about Science

## Risk

Everything we do (or not do) carries **risk**. Nothing is completely risk-free. New technologies and processes based on scientific advances often introduce new risks.

Risk is sometimes calculated by measuring the chance of something occurring in a large sample over a given period of time (**calculated risk**). This enables people to take informed decisions about whether the risk is worth taking. In order to decide, you have to balance the **benefit** (to individuals or groups) with the **consequences** of what could happen.

For example, deciding whether or not to have a vaccination involves weighing up the benefit (of being protected against a disease) against the risk (of side effects).

Risk which is associated with something that someone has chosen to do is easier to accept than risk which has been imposed on them.

HT Perception of risk changes depending on our personal experience (**perceived risk**). Familiar risks (e.g. smoking) tend to be underestimated, whilst unfamiliar risks (e.g. a new vaccination) and invisible or long-term risks (e.g. radiation) tend to be overestimated.

For example, many people underestimate the risk of getting type 2 diabetes from eating too much unhealthy food.

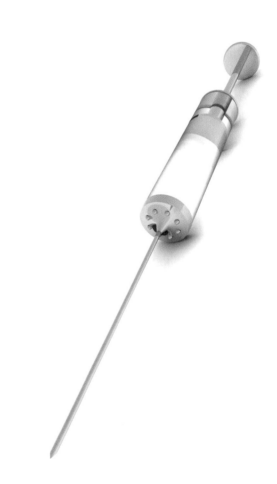

Governments and public bodies try to assess risk and create **policy** on what is and what isn't acceptable. This can be controversial, especially when the people who benefit most aren't the ones at risk.

## Making Decisions about Science and Technology

Science has helped to create **new technologies** that have improved the world, benefiting millions of people. However, there can be unintended **consequences** of new technologies, even many decades after they were first introduced. These could be related to the impact on the environment or to the quality of life.

When introducing new technologies, the potential benefits must be weighed up against the risks.

Sometimes unintended consequences affecting the environment can be identified. By applying the scientific method (making hypotheses, explanations and carrying out experiments), physicists can devise new ways of putting right the impact. Devising **life cycle assessments** helps scientists to try to minimise unintended consequences and ensure sustainability.

Some areas of physics could have a high potential risk to individuals or groups if they go wrong or if they're abused. In these areas the Government ensures that regulations are in place.

The scientific approach covers anything where data can be collected and used to test a hypothesis. It can't be used when evidence can't be collected (e.g. it can't test beliefs or values).

Just because something can be done doesn't mean that it should be done. Some areas of scientific research or the technologies resulting from them have **ethical issues** associated with them. This means that not all people will necessarily agree with it.

**Ethical decisions** have to be made, taking into account the views of everyone involved, whilst balancing the benefits and risks.

It's impossible to please everybody, so decisions are often made on the basis of which outcome will benefit most people. Within a culture there will also be some actions that are always right or wrong, no matter what the circumstances are.

# Contents

# Contents

Revised

## Unit A181

**4** Module P1: The Earth in the Universe

**14** Exam Practice Questions

**16** Module P2: Radiation and Life

**24** Exam Practice Questions

**26** Module P3: Sustainable Energy

**34** Exam Practice Questions

## Unit A182

**36** Module P4: Explaining Motion

**46** Exam Practice Questions

**48** Module P5: Electric Circuits

**56** Exam Practice Questions

**58** Module P6: Radioactive Materials

**66** Exam Practice Questions

## Unit A183

**68** Module P7: Further Physics – Studying the Universe

**86** Exam Practice Questions

**88** Answers

**92** Glossary of Key Words

**97** Index

# P1 The Earth in the Universe

## The Earth

When it first formed, the Earth was completely **molten** (hot liquid).

Scientists estimate the Earth is **4500 million** years old as it has to be older than its oldest rocks. The oldest rocks found on Earth are about 4000 million years old.

Studying rocks tells us more about the Earth's structure and how it has changed as a result of the following processes:

- **Erosion** – the Earth's surface is made of **rock layers**, one on top of another. The oldest is usually at the bottom. The layers are **compacted sediment**, produced by weathering and **erosion**. Erosion changes the surface over time.

- **Craters** – the Moon's surface is covered with **impact craters** from meteors. Meteors also hit the Earth but craters have been erased by erosion.
- **Mountain formation** – if new mountains weren't being formed, the Earth's surface would have eroded down to sea level.
- **Folding** – some rocks look as if they've been folded in half. This required huge force over a long time.

Further evidence of the Earth's age can be found by studying...

- **fossils** of plants and animals in **sedimentary rock layers**, which show how life has changed
- the **radioactivity** of rocks. A rock's **radioactivity** decreases over time and **radioactive dating** measures radiation levels to find out a rock's age.

## The Structure of the Earth

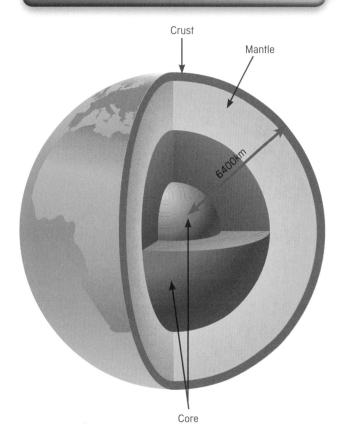

Crust
Mantle
6400km
Core

**Thin rocky crust:**
- Thickness varies between 10km and 100km.
- Oceanic crust lies beneath the oceans.
- Continental crust forms continents.

**The mantle:**
- Extends almost halfway to the centre of the Earth.
- Has a higher density, and different composition, than rock in the crust.
- Very hot, but under pressure.

**The core:**
- Accounts for over half of the Earth's radius.
- Made of nickel and iron, and has a liquid outer part and solid inner part.
- The decay of radioactive elements inside the Earth releases energy, keeping the interior hot.

**Key Words**      Erosion

## Continental Drift

**Continental drift** theory was proposed by **Wegener**. He saw that the continents had a jigsaw fit, with mountain ranges and rock patterns **matching up**.

There were also fossils of the same animals on different continents. He said that different continents had separated and drifted apart. Wegener also claimed that when two continents collided they forced each other upwards to make mountains.

Geologists didn't accept Wegener's theory because...
- he wasn't a geologist so was seen as an outsider
- the supporting evidence was limited
- it could be explained more simply, e.g. a bridge connecting continents had eroded over time
- the movement of the continents wasn't detectable.

Evidence from seafloor spreading finally convinced the scientific community that Wegener was correct. Through this **peer review process** it became an accepted theory.

**How The Earth Once Was**

Laurasia

Gondwanaland

**How The Earth Looks Today**

## Tectonic Plates

The Earth's crust is cracked into several large pieces called **tectonic plates**. The plates...
- float on the Earth's **mantle** as they're less dense
- can move apart, move towards, or slide past each other.

The lines where plates meet are called **plate boundaries**. **Volcanoes**, **earthquakes** and **mountain formations** normally occur at these plate boundaries.

Earthquakes near coastlines or at sea can often result in a **tsunami**.

North American plate

Eurasian plate

African plate

Nazca plate

South American plate

## Geohazards

A **geohazard** is a **natural hazard**, e.g. floods and hurricanes. Some have warning signs that give authorities time to evacuate the area, use sandbags, etc.

However, other geohazards strike without warning so precautionary measures need to be taken.

For example...
- buildings in earthquake zones are designed to withstand tremors
- authorities will often refuse planning permission in areas prone to flooding.

**Key Words**     Continental drift • Peer review • Tectonic plate • Geohazard

## Seafloor Spreading

The **mantle** is fairly solid just below the Earth's crust. Further down it's **liquid**.

**Convection currents** in the mantle cause **magma** to rise. The currents move the solid part of the mantle and the tectonic plates.

Where the plates are moving apart, magma reaches the surface and **hardens**, forming new areas of **oceanic crust** (seafloor) and pushing the existing floor outwards.

New crust is **continuously forming** at the crest of an oceanic ridge and old rock is pushed out. This causes seafloors to spread by a few centimetres a year.

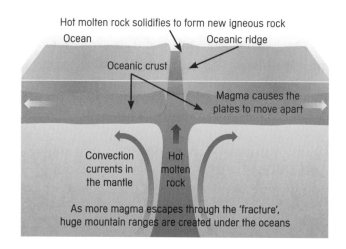

Hot molten rock solidifies to form new igneous rock

Ocean

Oceanic ridge

Oceanic crust

Magma causes the plates to move apart

Convection currents in the mantle

Hot molten rock

As more magma escapes through the 'fracture', huge mountain ranges are created under the oceans

## HT Plate Tectonics

The Earth has a **magnetic field**. It changes polarity every million years. Combined with seafloor spreading, this produces **rock stripes** of **alternating polarity**. Geologists can see how quickly crust is forming by the width of the stripes. This occurs at **constructive plate boundaries** where plates are moving apart.

When oceanic and continental plates **collide**, the denser oceanic plate is forced under the continental plate. This is subduction. The oceanic plate melts and molten rock can rise to form volcanoes. This occurs at **destructive plate boundaries**.

**Mountain ranges** form along colliding plate boundaries as sedimentary rock is forced up by the pressure created in a collision.

Earthquakes occur most frequently at plate boundaries:

1. The plates slide past each other or collide.
2. Pressure builds up as plates push on each other.
3. Eventually, **stored energy** is released and waves of energy spread from the **epicentre**.

Plate movement is crucial in the rock cycle:

- Old rock is destroyed through **subduction**.
- **Igneous rock** is formed when magma reaches the surface.
- Plate collisions can produce high temperatures and pressure, causing the rock to fold.
- **Sedimentary rock** becomes **metamorphic rock**.

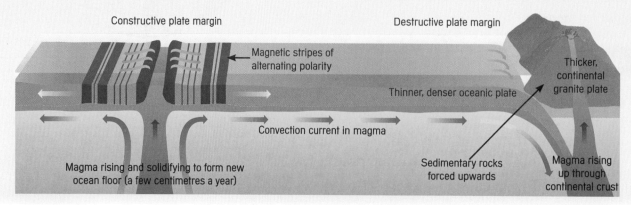

Constructive plate margin

Destructive plate margin

Magnetic stripes of alternating polarity

Thicker, continental granite plate

Thinner, denser oceanic plate

Convection current in magma

Magma rising and solidifying to form new ocean floor (a few centimetres a year)

Sedimentary rocks forced upwards

Magma rising up through continental crust

## Waves from Earthquakes

**Earthquakes** produce wave motions on the surface and inside the Earth. These waves can be detected by instruments located on the Earth's surface, such as a **seismograph**.

Two types of wave generated by earthquakes are...
- primary waves (P-waves)
- secondary waves (S-waves).

P-waves...
- travel faster than S-waves
- can travel through both liquids and solids
- can travel through the liquid region of the outer core of the Earth.

S-waves...
- can only travel through solids
- can't travel through the liquid region of the outer core of the Earth.

(HT) P-waves are **longitudinal waves** and S-waves are **transverse waves**.

P-waves and S-waves travel at different speeds in rocks of different density. If the rock has a high density, the waves travel faster.

The boundaries between the different types of rock lead to changes in the speed of P-waves and S-waves. This causes **refraction** or **reflection** of waves.

Measurements taken from **seismographs** at different points on the Earth's surface can be used to give evidence about the structure of the Earth.

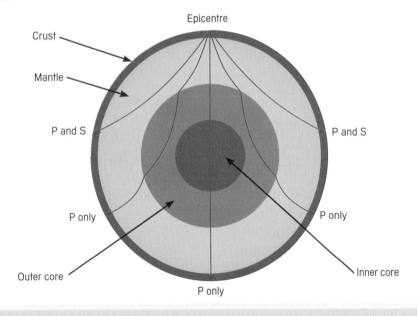

Epicentre
Crust
Mantle
P and S
P and S
P only
P only
Outer core
Inner core
P only

## Quick Test

1. Give three reasons why geologists didn't accept Wegener's theory.
2. What provides the heat in the Earth's core?
3. What evidence do scientists study to obtain information about the Earth's age?
4. What type of wave, generated by an earthquake, travels through the liquid outer core of the Earth?
5. (HT) In plate movement, old rock is destroyed by which process?
6. (HT) What two factors produce rock stripes of alternating polarity?

**Key Words**      Seismograph • Refraction

# P1 The Earth in the Universe

## Types of Wave

**Waves** are regular patterns of disturbance that transfer energy from one point to another without transferring particles of matter.

There are two types of wave:

- **Longitudinal**
- **Transverse**

In **longitudinal waves**, each particle…

- vibrates backwards and forwards about its normal position
- moves backwards and forwards in the same plane as the direction of wave movement.

**Sound** travels as longitudinal waves.

In **transverse waves**, each particle…

- vibrates up and down about its normal position
- moves up and down at right angles (90°) to the direction of wave movement.

**Light** and **water** ripples both travel as transverse waves. All electromagnetic waves travel as transverse waves.

In the diagrams opposite, the movement of coils in a slinky spring is used to represent the movement of particles in waves.

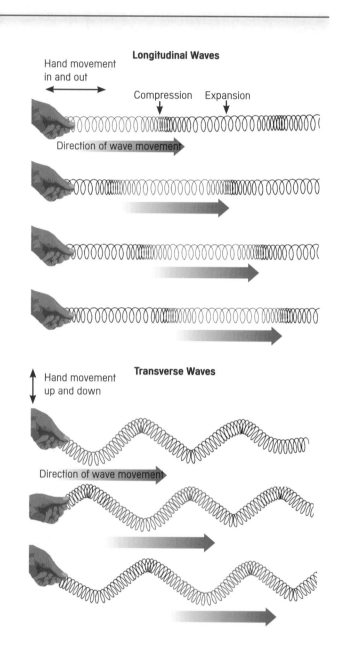

## Wave Features

All waves have several important features:

- **Amplitude** – the maximum disturbance caused by a wave, measured by the distance from a crest (or trough) of the wave to the undisturbed position.
- **Wavelength** – the distance between corresponding points on two adjacent disturbances.
- **Frequency** – the number of waves produced (or passing a particular point) in one second. Frequency is measured in **hertz** (Hz).

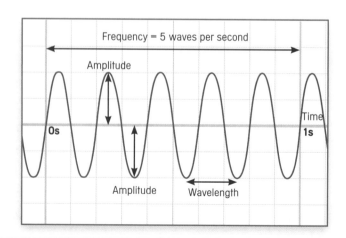

**Key Words**    Longitudinal wave • Transverse wave • Amplitude • Wavelength • Frequency

## Wave Speed and Frequency

If a wave travels at a constant speed…
- **increasing** its frequency will **decrease** its wavelength
- **decreasing** its frequency will **increase** its wavelength.

Frequency is inversely proportional to wavelength.

If a wave has a constant frequency…
- **decreasing** its wave speed will **decrease** its wavelength
- **increasing** its wave speed will **increase** its wavelength.

*N.B. The speed of a wave is usually independent of its frequency and amplitude.*

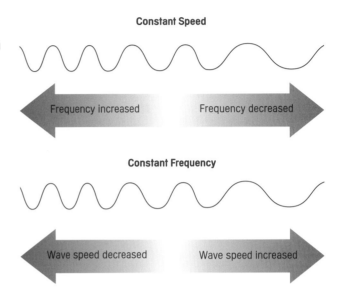

## The Wave Equation

Wave speed, frequency and wavelength are related by this formula:

$$\text{Wave speed (metres per second, m/s)} = \text{Frequency (hertz, Hz)} \times \text{Wavelength (metres, m)}$$

$$\frac{v}{f \times \lambda}$$

where *v* is wave speed, *f* is frequency and λ is wavelength

### Example

A tuning fork of frequency 480Hz produces sound waves with a wavelength of 70cm when it is tapped. What is the speed of the wave?

Wave speed = Frequency × Wavelength
= 480Hz × 0.7m
= **336m/s**

## Calculating the Distance a Wave Travels

This formula is used to calculate the distance a wave travels at a given speed in a certain time:

$$\text{Distance (metres, m)} = \text{Wave speed (metres per second, m/s)} \times \text{Time (seconds, s)}$$

(HT) You can work out the frequency or wavelength by rearranging the wave speed formula.

### Example

Radio 5 Live transmits on a frequency of 909 000Hz. If the speed of radio waves is 300 000 000m/s, on what wavelength does it transmit?

$$\text{Wavelength} = \frac{\text{Wave speed}}{\text{Frequency}}$$

$$= \frac{300\,000\,000\text{m/s}}{909\,000\text{Hz}}$$

$$= \textbf{330m}$$

## Quick Test

1. What type of wave is a sound wave?
2. A water wave has a frequency of 5 hertz and a wavelength of 0.1m. What is the speed of the wave?
3. What is a student describing if they tell you the number of waves produced each second?
4. (HT) A station broadcasts signals at a frequency of 30MHz. If the speed of light is $3 \times 10^8$ m/s, what is the wavelength?

## The Solar System

The **solar system** was formed about 5000 million years ago:

1. The solar system started as **dust** and **gas clouds**, pulled together by **gravity**.
2. This created intense heat. **Nuclear fusion** began and the Sun (a star) was born.
3. The remaining dust and gas formed smaller masses, which were **attracted** to the Sun…

The Sun is massive when compared with the planets and contains over 99% of the mass of the solar system.

Smaller masses in our solar system are…

- **planets** – eight large masses that orbit the Sun.
- **moons** – small masses that orbit planets.
- **asteroids** – small, rocky masses that orbit the Sun.
- **comets** – small, icy masses that orbit the Sun.
- **dwarf planets** – small masses (e.g. Pluto) orbiting the Sun.

Planets, moons and asteroids all move in **elliptical** (slightly squashed, circular) orbits.

Comets move in **highly elliptical** orbits. Earth takes **one year** to make a **complete orbit**.

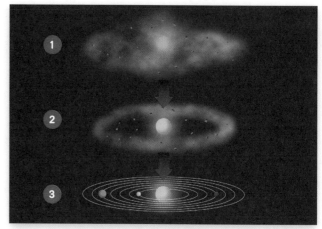

**Formation of the Solar System**

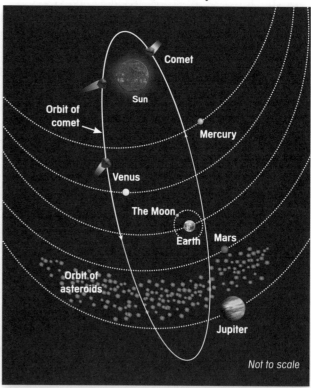

**Orbits in Part of the Solar System**

Comet

Orbit of comet

Sun

Mercury

Venus

The Moon

Earth

Mars

Orbit of asteroids

Jupiter

*Not to scale*

## The Sun

The Sun is only **500 million years older** than the Earth.

The Sun's energy comes from **nuclear fusion**:

1. Hydrogen atoms **fuse** together to produce an atom with a **larger mass**, i.e. a new chemical element.
2. **Binding energy** stored in hydrogen atoms is **released**.

All the chemical elements larger than helium were formed by nuclear fusion in earlier stars.

It's the **nuclei** of hydrogen atoms that fuse together during nuclear fusion.

## The Universe

The Universe is much older than the Sun, approximately **14 000 million years** old.

*Not to scale*

**The Universe** – contains billions of galaxies, with vast distances between them.

**Our Sun**

**Our star** – the Sun, 110 times wider than Earth

**Our galaxy**

**Our galaxy** – the Milky Way, 100 000 light-years across, containing at least 200 billion stars.

**Our planet** – the Earth, 12 800km in diameter

## The Speed of Light

Light travels at very high but **finite** (limited) speeds. If the distance is great enough, the **speed of light** can be measured.

The **speed of light** through space (a vacuum) is **300 000km/s** (around one million times faster than sound). Light from Earth takes just over one second to reach the Moon (approximately 384 400km away).

Sunlight takes eight minutes to reach Earth. When we look at the Sun we see it as it was eight minutes earlier.

Vast space distances are measured in **light-years**. One light-year is the distance light travels in one year (approximately 9500 billion km).

The nearest galaxy to the **Milky Way** is 2.2 million light-years away.

## Measuring Distances in Space

Distances are measured in **two** ways:

1. **Relative brightness** – the **dimmer** a star, the **further away** it is. However, brightness can vary so a star's distance is never certain.

2. **Parallax** – if you hold a finger at arm's length and close each eye in turn, your finger appears to move. The closer your finger, the more it seems to move. **Parallax** uses this idea to work out distance. Stars in the near distance appear to move against the background of distant stars. The closer they are, the more they appear to move. The further the star, the less accurate the measurement is.

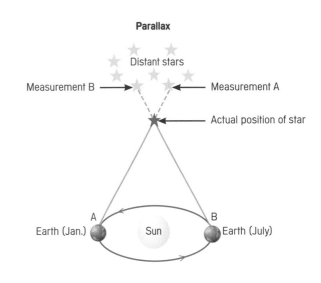

**Parallax**

Distant stars

Measurement B → ← Measurement A

Actual position of star

A B
Earth (Jan.)    Sun    Earth (July)

# P1 The Earth in the Universe

## Distant Stars

**Radiation** from stars tells us what we know about them. Types of radiation that stars produce include **visible light**, **ultraviolet** and **infrared**.

**Light pollution** is when electric lights on Earth make it difficult to see the stars. The Hubble Space Telescope orbits at a height of 600km, so it's not affected by this or other atmospheric conditions.

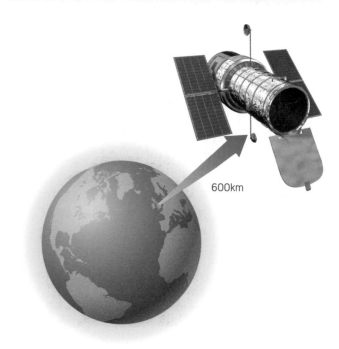

600km

## Other Galaxies

If a source of light is **moving away** from us, the wavelengths of light are **longer** than if the source is stationary.

Wavelengths of light from nearby galaxies are longer than scientists expect. This means the galaxies are **moving away** from us.

(HT) Observations made by **Edwin Hubble** showed that almost all galaxies are moving away from us and the further away they are, the faster they are moving away. He developed this into Hubble's Law, which states:

*The speed at which a galaxy is moving away is proportional to its distance from us.*

If all the galaxies are moving away from us, this must mean that the Universe is **expanding**.

If an electromagnetic wave appears to have a longer wavelength than it should have, then it's been **red shifted**. The object must therefore be moving away. The more the wavelengths are red shifted, the faster the object is moving away.

**Hydrogen Spectra from a Stationary Source**

**Hydrogen Spectra from a Star in a Galaxy Moving Away**

Look at the spectra above. The waves from a star in a galaxy moving away appear to have a longer wavelength than those from a stationary source.

(HT) They appear to be **red shifted**. The lines in the spectrum are displaced towards the red end of the spectrum.

## Relative Sizes in the Universe

The following measurements are listed in order of increasing size:

| Measurement | Relative Size |
|---|---|
| Diameter of the Earth | 12 742km |
| Diameter of the Sun | 110 times the diameter of the Earth |
| Size of the Earth's orbit | 107 times the diameter of the Sun |
| Distance of the Sun to the nearest star | 4 light-years |
| Size of the solar system | Several thousand light-years |
| Size of the Milky Way | 100 000 light-years |
| Distance of the Milky Way to the nearest galaxy | 2.2 million light-years |

## The Beginning and the End

The **Big Bang** theory says that the Universe began with a huge explosion 14 000 million years ago.

The future of the Universe is hard to predict because of the difficulties in measuring the very large distances involved, the motion of very distant objects and the assumptions made in interpreting observations.

HT A knowledge of the quantity of mass in the Universe is also required to predict the future.

If there **isn't enough** mass, the Universe will keep **expanding**. If there's **too much mass**, gravity will pull everything back together and the Universe will **collapse**.

**The Expansion of the Universe**

BANG!

## Quick Test

1 What is the difference between moons and asteroids?
2 What two methods are used to measure the distance of stars?
3 How is the wavelength of light changed if the source of light is moving away?
4 Why is it hard to predict the fate of the Universe?
5 HT How do spectra give evidence for red shift?
6 HT What is the relationship between the distance of galaxies and the speed at which they're moving away?

# P1 Exam Practice Questions

**1** A group of students is discussing Wegener's theory of continental drift.

**Toni**
The continents seem to fit together like a jigsaw.

**Charlie**
He used the periodic table.

**Tanya**
The rock patterns are the same on different continents.

**Ademola**
The bridge connecting the continents had eroded away over time.

**(a)** Which **two** students have made a statement that supports Wegener's theory?. **[1]**

......................................... and .........................................

**(b)** Which student makes a statement made by geologists who didn't accept Wegener's theory? **[1]**

.........................................................................................

**2** Major earthquakes occurred in the San Francisco Bay area in the following years:
1892, 1896, 1906, 1911, 1979, 1980, 1984, 1989, 2001, 2007

**(a)** Give two ways in which the local authority might protect the population from possible earthquakes. **[2]**

.........................................................................................

.........................................................................................

**(b)** A scientist looks at the data and concludes that the next earthquake will be in 2013. Which of the conclusions below would have been more sensible? Put ticks (✓) in the boxes next to the **two** best answers. **[2]**

There were no major earthquakes for 68 years in San Francisco Bay. ⬭

Earthquakes occur at least once every 10 years. ⬭

San Francisco lies near a fault line. ⬭

Scientists might have missed earthquakes before 1979. ⬭

**3** Which of the following statements are true? Put ticks (✓) next to the **three** correct statements. **[3]**

The solar system is 5000 million years old. ⬭

The Earth's crust floats on a liquid mantle. ⬭

The Sun was born when nuclear fusion started in gas and dust clouds pulled together by gravity. ⬭

Pluto is no longer considered to be a planet. ⬭

The Sun is only 600 million years older than the Earth. ⬭

**4** Below are three terms used to describe waves and three statements explaining their meaning. Draw a straight line from each term to join it to the correct statement. **[2]**

| Amplitude | The distance between the corresponding points on two adjacent cycles |
|---|---|
| Frequency | The number of waves made per second by a source |
| Wavelength | A measurement of how much energy a wave carries |

**5** A 3m wave has a frequency of 12Hz. At what speed is it travelling? **[1]**

**HT 6** This question is about earthquakes and how they're detected.

Earthquakes generate two types of wave that can be detected by instruments at other locations on the Earth's surface. Explain the difference between the two types of wave produced, why some regions might only detect one type of wave and how these waves can be used to give evidence for the structure of the Earth. **[6]**

*The quality of written communication will be assessed in your answer to this question.*

**7** Scientists often say that light from distant galaxies is **red shifted**.

**(a)** What do you understand by the term 'red shift'? **[2]**

**(b)** What evidence supported the idea that the Universe was expanding. **[2]**

**(c)** Why is it difficult to measure the mass of the Universe? **[2]**

**8** How do scientists explain the pattern of magnetism of seafloor rocks on either side of oceanic ridges? **[2]**

# P2 Radiation and Life

## The Electromagnetic Spectrum

The **electromagnetic spectrum** is a family of seven radiations, including **visible light**.

A **beam** of electromagnetic radiation contains '**packets**' of energy called **photons**.

The higher the frequency of an electromagnetic radiation, the more energy is transferred by each photon. All electromagnetic radiation travels at the same finite speed of 300000km/s through space (a vacuum).

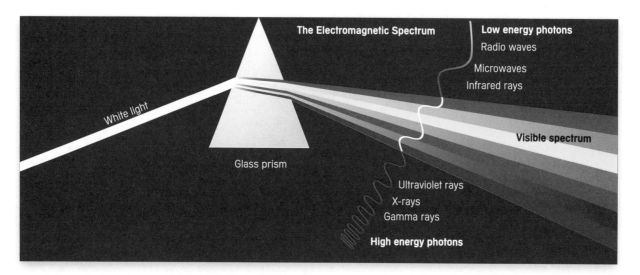

## Transmitting Radiation

The general model of radiation shows how energy travels from a **source** that **emits** radiation, to a **detector** that **absorbs** radiation.

On the journey from **emitter** to **detector**, materials can **transmit**, **reflect** or **absorb** radiation.

For example, clouds absorb and reflect the Sun's energy, so on a cloudy day we receive less light than on a clearer day.

| Emitter | Type of Wave | Detector |
|---|---|---|
| TV transmitter | Radio waves | TV aerial |
| Mobile phone mast | Microwaves | Mobile phone |
| Remote control | Infrared waves | Television |
| The Sun | Light | The eye |
| Ultraviolet lamp | Ultraviolet rays | The skin |
| X-ray machine | X-rays | Photographic plate |
| Some stars (e.g. supernova) | Gamma rays | Gamma ray telescope |

## Intensity and Heat

The **intensity** of electromagnetic radiation is the energy arriving at a **square metre of surface per second**.

Intensity depends on the number of photons delivered per second and the amount of energy each packet contains, i.e. the photon energy.

The intensity of a beam **decreases** with distance, so the further from a source you are, the lower the intensity.

When a material absorbs radiation, heat is created. The amount of heat created depends on...
- the **intensity** of the radiation beam
- the **duration** of the exposure.

**Key Words**     Electromagnetic spectrum • Photon

## HT Intensity and Heat (Cont.)

The decrease in the intensity of radiation with distance is due to three factors:

- Photons **spread out** as they travel.
- Some photons are **absorbed** by particles in the substances they pass through.
- Some photons are **reflected** and **scattered** by other particles.

These factors **combine** to reduce the number of photons arriving per second at a detector. This results in a **lower measured intensity**.

## Ionising Radiation

Ionising radiation (electromagnetic radiation with a high photon energy) can break molecules into bits called **ions**. **Ultraviolet** radiation, **X-rays** and **gamma rays** are examples of ionising radiation.

HT Ions are **very reactive** and can easily take part in other chemical reactions.

Electromagnetic radiations that are ionising have a high enough photon energy to remove an electron from an atom or molecule.

## Cell Damage

Radiation **damages** living cells in different ways:

- The heating effect can damage the skin, e.g. sunburn.
- Ionising radiation can age the skin. It can also **mutate** DNA, which can lead to cancer.
- Different amounts of exposure can cause different effects, e.g. high intensity ionising radiation can destroy cells, leading to **radiation poisoning**.

**Microwaves** can heat materials by causing the water particles to vibrate. There may be a health **risk** from the low intensity microwaves of mobile phones and masts, but this is disputed. One study found no link from short-term use but other studies have found some correlation.

**Radiation Damage**

Ionising radiation source

The irradiated cell may...

...suffer no damage.

...mutate, which can lead to cancer.

...die, leading to burns, sickness and even death.

# P2 Radiation and Life

## Radiation Protection

Microwave ovens have a metal case and a wire screen in the door to absorb microwaves and stop too much radiation escaping.

Other **physical barriers** are used to protect people:
- X-ray technicians use **lead screens**.
- Sunscreens and clothing can absorb ultraviolet radiation to help prevent skin cancer.

- Nuclear reactors are encased in thick lead and concrete.

Some radioactive materials emit ionising gamma radiation all the time. People going into areas of high radiation must wear a **radiation suit** as a shield and have a **radiation dose monitor**.

## The Sun and the Ozone Layer

All objects emit electromagnetic radiation with a principal frequency that increases with temperature.

Light radiation from the Sun…
- warms the Earth's surface when it's absorbed
- is used by plants for **photosynthesis**.

Photosynthesis **counteracts** respiration – it removes carbon dioxide and adds oxygen.

The **ozone layer** is a thin layer of gas in the Earth's upper atmosphere. It absorbs some of the Sun's ultraviolet radiation before it reaches Earth.

Without the ozone layer, the amount of radiation reaching the Earth would be **very harmful**. Living organisms, especially animals, would suffer cell damage.

(HT) The energy from ultraviolet radiation causes chemical changes in the upper atmosphere when it's absorbed by the ozone layer. These changes are **reversible**.

## The Greenhouse Effect

The Earth emits electromagnetic radiation into space. Gases in the atmosphere absorb some of the radiation and this keeps the Earth warmer than it would otherwise be. This is known as the **greenhouse effect**.

The atmosphere also only allows some of the electromagnetic radiation emitted by the Sun to pass through.

Carbon dioxide (a **greenhouse gas**) makes up a small amount of the Earth's atmosphere. The amount has been steadily rising in the last 200 years.

Other greenhouse gases include…
- **water vapour**
- trace amounts of **methane**.

(HT) Radiation emitted by the Earth has a lower principal frequency than that emitted by the Sun.

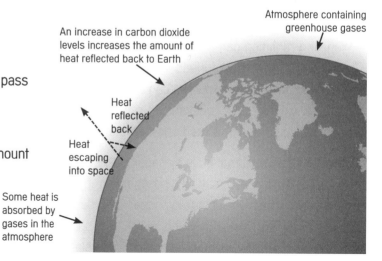

Atmosphere containing greenhouse gases

An increase in carbon dioxide levels increases the amount of heat reflected back to Earth

Heat reflected back

Heat escaping into space

Some heat is absorbed by gases in the atmosphere

Photosynthesis • Ozone layer • Greenhouse effect

## The Carbon Cycle

The **carbon cycle** is an example of a balanced system.

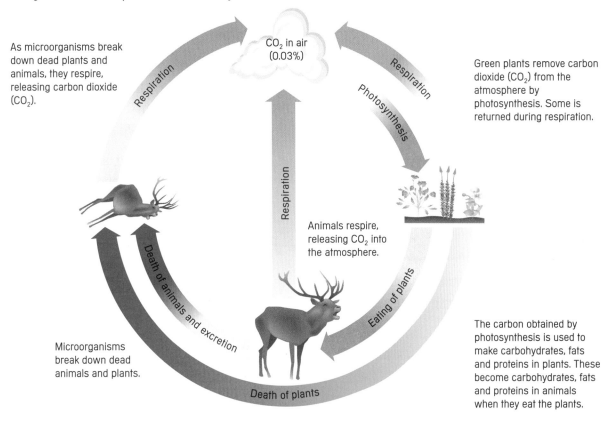

As microorganisms break down dead plants and animals, they respire, releasing carbon dioxide ($CO_2$).

Respiration

CO₂ in air (0.03%)

Respiration

Photosynthesis

Green plants remove carbon dioxide ($CO_2$) from the atmosphere by photosynthesis. Some is returned during respiration.

Respiration

Animals respire, releasing $CO_2$ into the atmosphere.

Eating of plants

Death of animals and excretion

Microorganisms break down dead animals and plants.

Death of plants

The carbon obtained by photosynthesis is used to make carbohydrates, fats and proteins in plants. These become carbohydrates, fats and proteins in animals when they eat the plants.

## Using the Carbon Cycle

The carbon cycle can be used to explain several points:

- Carbon dioxide ($CO_2$) levels in the Earth's atmosphere remained roughly **constant** for thousands of years because it was constantly being **recycled** by plants and animals.
- **Decomposers** are important microorganisms that break down dead material and release $CO_2$.
- $CO_2$ levels in the atmosphere have been steadily increasing, largely due to human activity, e.g. burning **fossil fuels** and **deforestation**.
- Burning fossil fuels releases carbon that was removed from the atmosphere millions of years ago and had been 'locked up' ever since.
- Burning forests not only releases carbon, but also reduces the number of plants removing $CO_2$ from the atmosphere.

## Quick Test

1. Which photon transfers the most energy: infrared or ultraviolet?
2. Name three ionising radiations.
3. Give two ways in which radiation can damage cells.
4. What is the ozone layer?
5. HT How does the radiation emitted by the Earth compare with that emitted by the Sun?
6. HT Give three reasons why the intensity of a beam of photons decreases with distance.

# P2 Radiation and Life

## Global Warming

The increase in greenhouse gases causes a rise in the amount of radiation from the Sun that is absorbed in the Earth's atmosphere. This causes the Earth's temperature to increase, an effect known as **global warming**, which may lead to…

- **climate change** – crops may not be able to grow in some areas
- **extreme weather**, e.g. hurricanes
- **rising sea levels** – melting ice caps and higher sea temperatures may cause sea levels to rise, flooding low-lying land.

**HT** Data about the Earth's changing temperature is collected and used with climate models to look for **patterns** in the possible causes of **global warming**.

These computer models show that one of the main global warming factors is the rise in carbon dioxide levels in the atmosphere, providing evidence that human activity is to blame.

Increased convection and larger amounts of water vapour in the hotter atmosphere could result in more extreme weather events.

## Analogue Signals

Information can be superimposed onto an electromagnetic **carrier wave** to create a signal.

In amplitude modulation or frequency modulation (AM or FM), the amplitude or frequency of the carrier wave is changed by the input signal.

With frequency modulation the input signal causes the frequency of the carrier wave to change.

With amplitude modulation the input signal causes the amplitude of the carrier wave to change.

In both of these cases, the signal is called an **analogue** signal because it varies in exactly the same way as the information it's carrying. Analogue signals can have almost any value.

**Frequency Modulation**

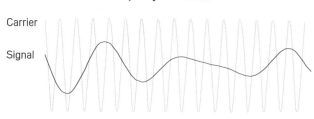

Carrier

Signal

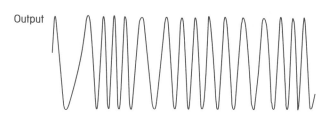

Output

**Amplitude Modulation**

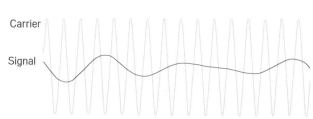

Carrier

Signal

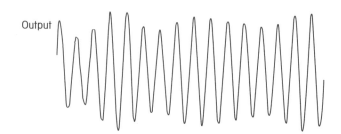

Output

**Global warming • Analogue**

## Uses of Electromagnetic Waves

Different electromagnetic waves have **different frequencies**.

They can be used for different purposes depending on how much they are **reflected**, **absorbed** or **transmitted** by different materials.

Their signals can be carried by...
- radio waves and microwaves (through the Earth's atmosphere and space)
- light waves and infrared waves (through optical fibres).

| Electromagnetic Waves | Properties and Uses |
|---|---|
| Radio waves | • They are used for transmitting radio and television programmes because they aren't strongly absorbed by the atmosphere. |
| Microwaves | • They are reflected well by metals, so satellite dishes are made of metal.<br>• Some microwave frequencies are strongly absorbed by water molecules, so they are used to heat objects containing water.<br>• Some microwaves aren't strongly absorbed by the atmosphere, so they can carry TV and radio signals. |
| Visible light and infrared | • They travel huge distances down optic fibres without becoming significantly weaker, so they are very useful for carrying information.<br>• They can be easily boosted at intervals along the optical fibre. |
| X-rays | • They are absorbed by dense materials, so they are used to produce shadow pictures of bones and to 'see' inside luggage at airport security checks. |

## Digital Signals

Information, including sound, can also be transmitted **digitally**.

The signal is converted into a digital code that uses just two symbols (0 and 1), which can then be transmitted as a series of short bursts of waves called **pulses** (0 = no pulse, i.e. off, 1 = pulse, i.e. on). Pulses are produced by switching the electromagnetic carrier wave on and off.

When the digital signal is received, the pulses are decoded to produce a copy of the original sound wave or image.

**Flat-screen TV used to Display Pictures Carried by Digital Signals**

## Benefits of Digital Signals

Both digital and analogue signals...
- become weaker (their amplitude becomes smaller) as they travel, so they may have to be **amplified** at selected intervals
- can pick up random variations, called **noise**, which reduce the quality of the sound.

When a signal is amplified, any noise which has been picked up is also amplified.

Digital signals can travel long distances at a **higher quality** than analogue signals. This is because...
- **analogue signals** can have many different values, so it's hard to distinguish between noise and the original signal. This means that noise can't be completely removed.
- **digital signals** only have two states, on (1) or off (0), so they can still be recognised despite any noise that's picked up. This means that any **interference** can be removed.

(HT) When digital signals carry noise, it's clear which parts of the signal represent 1 and 0, so the signal can be regenerated without the noise.

**A Sent Analogue Signal**

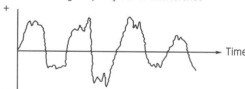

**A Received Analogue Signal**
Poor signal quality due to interference

**A Sent Digital Signal**

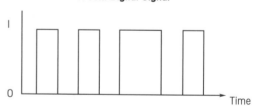

**A Received Digital Signal**
High signal quality as interference is easily removed

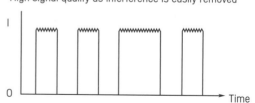

## Storing Information

A **bit** is one piece of information represented as either 1 or 0. One **byte** is equal to eight bits of information.

In a digital mobile phone picture, each pixel needs eight bits of information or one byte. The more pixels in the picture...
- the more bytes of information there are
- the higher the quality of the picture.

The picture will then be stored on a memory card and the amount of information stored is measured in **bytes**.

Digital music is also stored on a CD in the form of **bytes**. There is a series of pits, each read by a laser as 1 (a bit), arranged in a spiral on the surface. In between are flat surfaces read as 0. The series of bits is then converted back into analogue form giving a high quality signal.

## Using Digital Information

The advantage of transmitting information using digital signals is that...
- information can be stored, e.g. on hard drive, CD, DVD or **memory stick**
- information can be processed by computer, e.g. for spell checking, photo editing or music editing.

| Type of Information Transmitted | How a Computer can be used to Process and Store Information |
|---|---|
| Digital pictures | • Use of photo-editing software to manipulate images<br>• Store on hard drive, CD or memory stick |
| Music in MP3 / WAV format | • Remove noise, amplify and edit signals<br>• Store on hard drive, CD or memory stick |

## Quick Test

1. What change in the Earth's atmosphere causes global warming?
2. Why is optic fibre useful when sending infrared and light radiation?
3. What is noise?
4. How is an analogue signal different from a digital one?
5. HT Why doesn't noise affect digital signals?
6. HT How is data, collected about the Earth's changing temperature, used?

# P2 Exam Practice Questions

1. Which of the following statements is **not true**? Put a tick (✓) in the box next to the answer. **[1]**

   Radiation may affect another object some distance away if it's absorbed. ⬭

   X-rays have a shorter wavelength than gamma rays. ⬭

   A beam of electromagnetic radiation transfers energy in packets called photons. ⬭

   Radiation travelling outwards from a source can be reflected, transmitted or absorbed by material it encounters. ⬭

2. The students below are making statements about the use of the electromagnetic spectrum.

   **Deqa**
   My dentist took X-rays of my jaw.

   **Bola**
   My mobile uses microwaves.

   **Evelyn**
   I used ultraviolet to test for forgeries.

   **Thomas**
   I used a hand control emitting infrared.

   **(a)** Which students are talking about ionising radiation? Put ticks (✓) in the boxes next to the **two** correct names.

   Deqa ⬭     Bola ⬭     Evelyn ⬭     Thomas ⬭     **[1]**

   **(b)** Which student mentions radiation with the highest frequency? Put a tick (✓) in the box next to the correct name. **[1]**

   Deqa ⬭     Bola ⬭     Evelyn ⬭     Thomas ⬭

3. The concentration of carbon dioxide in the air was measured on a mountain in Hawaii. The results are shown below:

   | Year | 1958 | 1968 | 1983 | 1998 | 2003 | 2008 |
   |---|---|---|---|---|---|---|
   | Concentration of $CO_2$ (ppm) | 1.0 | 1.8 | 2.4 | 3.0 | 3.3 | 4.1 |

   Kirsty looked at the data and wrote down two statements. The first concluded the link between the two variables and the other about how the data can be used. What might she have written down? **[2]**

   ..........................................................................................................................................................

   ..........................................................................................................................................................

4. Sajida measured the temperature of a beaker of water after it had been placed in a microwave oven, which was switched on for 10 seconds. She then wrote down five statements. Put ticks (✓) in the boxes next to the **two** correct statements. **[2]**

   Water molecules strongly absorb some microwave wavelengths. ⬭

   The heating effect of absorbed radiation isn't linked to the intensity. ⬭

   If I had put sunscreen on the outside of the beaker, the temperature wouldn't have gone up. ⬭

   Microwaves from mobile phones must be a health risk. ⬭

   Microwaves in microwave ovens have a different wavelength to the ones used by mobile phones. ⬭

**5** **(a)** Does the diagram below show an **analogue signal** or a **digital signal**? ......................................... **[1]**

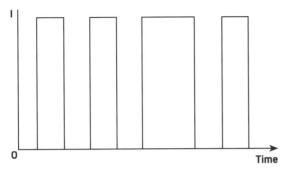

**(b)** Explain why digital signals are usually of better quality than analogue signals. **[2]**

.....................................................................................................................................................

.....................................................................................................................................................

**(c)** Name three ways in which digital signals can be stored. **[3]**

.....................................................................................................................................................

.....................................................................................................................................................

.....................................................................................................................................................

**HT** **6** Leading scientists are worried about the causes and effects of climate change.

**(a)** How does the use of computer climate models provide evidence that human activities are causing global warming? **[6]**

🖉 *The quality of written communication will be assessed in your answer to this question.*

.....................................................................................................................................................

.....................................................................................................................................................

.....................................................................................................................................................

.....................................................................................................................................................

.....................................................................................................................................................

.....................................................................................................................................................

.....................................................................................................................................................

**(b)** Give two ways in which global warming might result in more extreme weather events. **[2]**

.....................................................................................................................................................

.....................................................................................................................................................

**7** Explain why a signal, which has been affected by noise, can be recovered more easily if it's digital than if it's an analogue signal. **[2]**

.....................................................................................................................................................

.....................................................................................................................................................

.....................................................................................................................................................

# P3 Sustainable Energy

## Electricity

**Electricity** is a **secondary** energy source. This means it's generated from another energy source, e.g. coal, nuclear power, etc.

Electricity is a very useful energy source as it can be easily transmitted over long distances and used in many ways.

## Generating Electricity

The main primary energy sources that humans use are fossil fuels (oil, coal, gas), nuclear fuels, biofuel (e.g. wood), wind, waves and radiation from the Sun. To generate electricity, fuel is burned to produce heat:

1 The heat is used to boil water, which produces **steam**.

2 The steam drives the **turbines**, which power the **generators**.

3 Electricity produced in the generators is sent to a step-up **transformer** and then to the **National Grid**.

4 Electricity is distributed to homes and businesses through the National Grid at high **voltages** to reduce energy losses.

5 The high voltages are stepped down by a transformer to the mains supply voltage in our homes of 230V.

Power stations that burn fossil fuels like coal produce carbon dioxide, a greenhouse gas. This contributes to global warming and climate change.

Nuclear power stations release energy owing to changes in the **nucleus** of **radioactive** substances. They don't produce carbon dioxide but they do produce radioactive waste.

Nuclear waste emits ionising radiation. When handling radioactive material, there is a danger of being exposed to a radiation source outside your body. This is called **irradiation**.

If any part of a radiation source was to get on your clothes or enter your body, you would become **contaminated**. This would continually expose you to dangerous ionising radiation and would be a much greater threat to your health than a short period of irradiation from a radioactive source. It could cause damage to living cells, eventually leading to cancer or cell death.

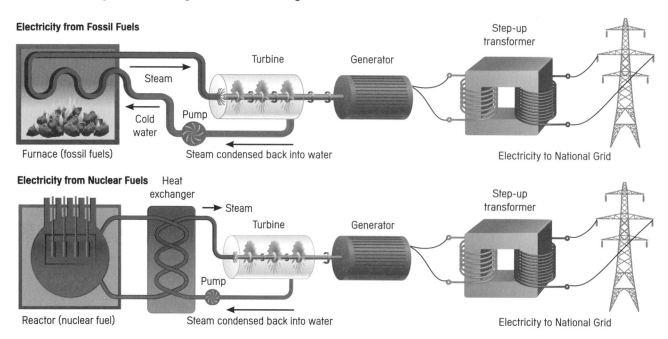

**Electricity from Fossil Fuels**

Turbine — Generator — Step-up transformer

Steam

Cold water — Pump

Furnace (fossil fuels)

Steam condensed back into water

Electricity to National Grid

**Electricity from Nuclear Fuels**

Heat exchanger — Steam — Turbine — Generator — Step-up transformer

Pump

Reactor (nuclear fuel)

Steam condensed back into water

Electricity to National Grid

**Key Words** Transformer • National Grid • Voltage • Nucleus • Radioactive • Irradiation • Contamination

## Sankey Diagrams

Energy is lost at every stage of the process of electricity generation.

**Sankey diagrams** can be used to show the generation and distribution of electricity, including the efficiency of **energy transfers**.

The Sankey diagram shows that from the energy put into the power station, almost half is lost to the surroundings (mostly as heat) before the electricity even reaches the home. Further energy is lost during energy transfers in the home when the electricity is used.

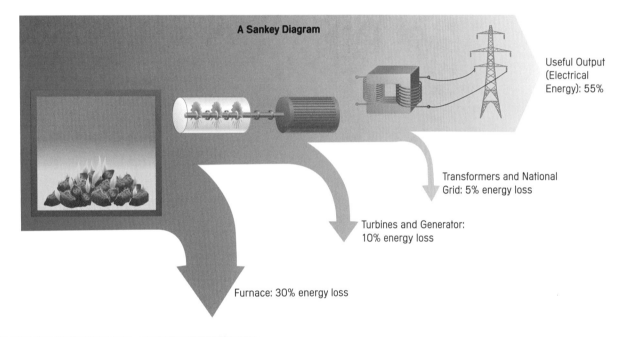

**A Sankey Diagram**

Input Chemical Energy of Fuel: 100%

Useful Output (Electrical Energy): 55%

Transformers and National Grid: 5% energy loss

Turbines and Generator: 10% energy loss

Furnace: 30% energy loss

## Renewable Energy

Conventional energy supplies are running out, and both nuclear and fossil fuels cause environmental damage. The burning of fossil fuels releases carbon dioxide into the atmosphere, contributing to global warming and climate change. This means that **alternative energy sources** are becoming more important.

Alternative ways to generate electricity include…
* wind
* waves
* hydroelectric power
* biofuel (e.g. wood)
* solar power
* geothermal.

These **renewable** energy sources are **primary energy sources** and will not run out like fossil fuels.

## Wind Turbines

An example of a **renewable energy** source is **wind turbines**. The force of the wind turns the blades of the wind turbine, which provides power to a generator.

The amount of electricity produced is small. It would need hundreds of wind turbines to replace a conventional power station. However, once built, they provide **free energy** as long as the wind is blowing.

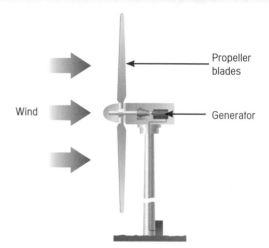

Wind

Propeller blades

Generator

A Wind Farm

## Hydroelectric Dam

**Hydroelectric dams** are another example of a renewable energy source. Water stored in the **reservoir** flows down pipes and turns the turbines. This powers the generators and produces electricity.

Large areas of land may need to be flooded to build **hydroelectric stations**. However, once built, they provide large amounts of reliable, fairly cheap energy.

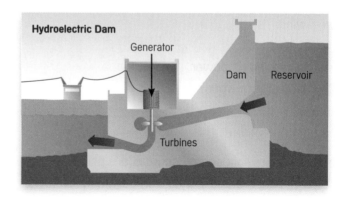

Hydroelectric Dam

Generator

Dam    Reservoir

Turbines

## The Generator

A **generator** is used to produce electricity when a magnet is made to rotate near a coil. In large generators the magnet is an electromagnet.

A generator can be driven by another energy source. Burning a fossil fuel can be used to heat water and produce steam to drive a **turbine** and generator. The generator can also be driven by an alternative energy source such as wind or water turbine. The greater the current supplied by a generator, the more primary fuel it uses each second.

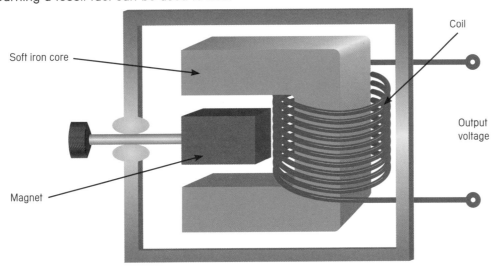

Soft iron core

Coil

Output voltage

Magnet

## The Use of a Generator in a Hydroelectric Power Station

The diagram opposite shows the energy changes in a hydroelectric power station when a generator is driven directly by the flow of water through a series of turbine blades.

The kinetic energy of the water causes the turbine blades to rotate.

The generator converts kinetic energy into electrical energy. This electrical energy can be transferred to homes and factories via the National Grid.

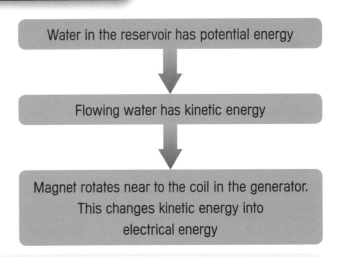

Water in the reservoir has potential energy

Flowing water has kinetic energy

Magnet rotates near to the coil in the generator. This changes kinetic energy into electrical energy

## Quick Test

1. Why is electricity distributed through the National Grid at high voltage?
2. Name five primary energy sources used to generate electricity.
3. The burning of fossil fuels releases carbon dioxide into the atmosphere. What two problems does this contribute to?
4. How is a voltage induced between the ends of a coil?
5. What are the three forms of energy that are involved in a hydroelectric power station?

# P3 Sustainable Energy

## Power

When charge flows through a component, **energy is transferred** to the component and lost to the environment.

**Power** is a measure of the rate of energy transfer and is measured in watts (W).

You can calculate power using the following formula:

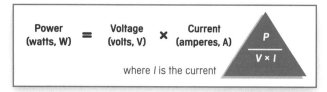

where *I* is the current

### Example
An electric motor works at a current of 3A and a potential difference of 24V. What is the power of the motor?

Power = Potential difference × Current

$\quad$ = 24V × 3A

$\quad$ = **72W**

(HT) You can work out the potential difference or current by rearranging the power formula.

### Example
A 40W lamp works at a current of 0.18A. What is the potential difference?

$$\text{Potential difference} = \frac{\text{Power}}{\text{Current}} = \frac{40W}{0.18A} = \textbf{222V}$$

## Energy

**Energy** is measured in **joules**. A joule is a very small amount of energy, so a domestic electricity meter measures the energy transfer in **kilowatt hours**.

You can calculate energy transfer in joules and kilowatt hours using the following formula:

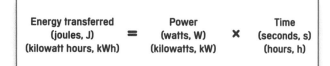

### Example 1
A 30W light bulb is switched on for 45 seconds. What is the energy transferred in joules?

Energy transferred = Power × Time

$\quad$ = 30W × 45s

$\quad$ = **1350J**

### Example 2
A 2000W electric hot plate is switched on for 90 minutes. What is the energy transferred in kWh?

Energy transferred = 2kW × 1.5h

$\quad$ = **3kWh**

(HT) You can work out the power or time by rearranging the energy transfer formula. Power is the rate at which an appliance or device transfers energy.

### Example
A hairdryer is switched on for 6 minutes and the total energy transferred is 0.2kWh. What is the power rating of the hairdryer?

$$\text{Power} = \frac{\text{Energy transferred}}{\text{Time}} = \frac{0.2kWh}{0.1h} = \textbf{2kW}$$

## Cost of Electricity

If you know the power, time and cost per kilowatt hour, you can calculate the cost of the electrical energy used. The formula is as follows:

| Total cost | = | Number of units (kWh) | ✕ | Cost per unit |

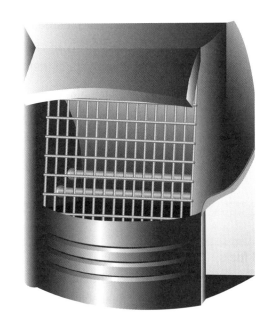

### Example

A 2000W electric fire is switched on for 30 minutes. How much does it cost if electricity is 8p per unit (kWh)?

Energy transferred = 2kW × 0.5h

= 1kWh (or 1 unit)

Cost = 1 × 8p

= **8p**

## Efficiency of Appliances

The greater the proportion of energy that's usefully transferred, the more **efficient** the appliance is.

You can calculate **efficiency** using this formula:

$$\text{Efficiency (\%)} = \frac{\text{Energy usefully transferred}}{\text{Total energy supplied}} \times 100$$

| Electrical Appliance | Energy In | Useful Energy Out | Efficiency |
|---|---|---|---|
| Light bulb | 100 joules/s | Light: 20 joules/s | $\frac{20}{100} \times 100\%$ = **20%** |
| Kettle | 2000 joules/s | Heat (in water): 1800 joules/s | $\frac{1800}{2000} \times 100\%$ = **90%** |
| Electric motor | 500 joules/s | Kinetic: 300 joules/s | $\frac{300}{500} \times 100\%$ = **60%** |
| Television | 200 joules/s | Light: 20 joules/s Sound: 30 joules/s | $\frac{50}{200} \times 100\%$ = **25%** |

# P3 Sustainable Energy

The demand for energy is continually increasing. This raises issues about the availability of energy sources and the environmental effects of them.

There are advantages and disadvantages to consider when using any primary energy source to generate electricity.

When comparing energy sources for generating electricity, the factors used to assess which source is the most favourable are **efficiency**, **cost** and **environmental damage**.

HT **Power output** and **lifetime** (how long a source lasts for) can also be assessed when comparing energy sources.

| Energy Source | Advantages | Disadvantages | Set-up Cost | HT Power Output |
|---|---|---|---|---|
| **Fossil fuels** | • High energy output<br>• Easily distributed<br>• Readily available<br>• Can be used anywhere<br>• Efficient<br>• Convenient | • Non renewable<br>• Burning generates greenhouse gases<br>• Obtaining fuels damages the environment<br>• Contributes to acid rain<br>• Emissions from the transport of fuel | High | High |
| **Nuclear** | • Reliable<br>• No greenhouse gases<br>• Convenient<br>• Efficient<br>• High energy output | • Disposal of nuclear waste is difficult and needs specialist handling<br>• It's expensive to remove spent fuel and send it for processing<br>• Threat of damage to the environment | Very high | High |
| **Biofuel** | • Renewable<br>• Inexhaustible supply | • Needs a large area of land to produce<br>• Burning leads to greenhouse gases<br>• Expensive to produce (labour, machinery) | Medium | Medium |
| **Solar** | • Renewable<br>• No greenhouse gases<br>• No solid or liquid waste | • Expensive and inefficient<br>• Needs a large surface area for panels<br>• Intensity of solar energy isn't consistent | High | Low |
| **Wind** | • Renewable<br>• No greenhouse gases<br>• No solid or liquid waste | • Expensive<br>• Noisy and spoils the view<br>• Needs large number of turbines to match a power station's output<br>• Variable output daily | High | Low |
| **Water (waves, hydroelectricity, tidal)** | • Renewable<br>• Reliable<br>• No greenhouse gases | • Expensive<br>• Environmental damage to the location<br>• Limited locations available<br>• Changes the ecosystem through flooding | High | High |
| **Geothermal** | • Renewable<br>• Small emission of greenhouse gases | • Expensive to drill for suitable sites<br>• Limited locations | High | Medium |

## Reducing Energy Demands

To save on energy consumption...
- **energy losses** need to be **reduced**
- the percentage of **useful energy** obtained from a source needs to be **increased**.

Energy losses in the home can be reduced by...
- installing double or triple-glazed windows
- cutting out draughts around doors, windows and skirting boards
- installing at least 270mm of loft **insulation**
- using energy-saving light bulbs
- switching off appliances (i.e. not leaving them on standby) when not required
- replacing old appliances with more efficient, newer models.

Energy can be saved both at home and at work by making a few changes, as shown below.

| In the Home | In the Workplace | National Context |
|---|---|---|
| • More efficient appliances, e.g. a condensing boiler could save £190 per year<br>• Double glazing – possible savings of £130 per year<br>• Loft insulation – possible savings of £145 per year<br>• Cavity wall insulation – possible savings of £110 per year<br>• Draught-proof rooms – possible savings of £25 per year | • Cleaning air conditioner filters – can save 5% of the energy used in running the system<br>• Using low-energy light bulbs<br>• Roof insulation / cavity wall insulation in modern buildings<br>• Use of efficient, modern, low-energy machinery<br>• Use of modern, efficient vehicles for transport of goods | • Replacing old houses with new efficient ones<br>• Increased use of public transport<br>• More efficient trains and buses<br>• Encourage more widespread recycling<br>• Encourage car sharing and fewer journeys |

## HT The National Need for a Mix of Energy Sources

To ensure a security of electricity supply nationally, we need a **mix of energy sources**.

By 2015, Britain is expected to import nearly 80% of the gas it needs, compared with 40% in 2011. Relying on imported primary energy sources is a concern. There are political and expense issues to consider.

Many nuclear power stations are coming to the end of their useful lives and will need to be replaced soon.

There are also restrictions on many coal-fired plants because of tough new European emissions standards.

Electricity from alternative energy sources still only provides a small amount of energy supplies. This includes wind, solar and hydroelectric energy. New wind farms are being built at sea and other alternative sources, such as wave and tidal energy sources, are being seriously considered. This indicates the importance of not relying on one or two main sources of electricity.

## Quick Test

1. How much energy is transferred by a 60W lamp in 3 seconds?
2. How efficient is an electric motor that uses 400J/s to give 100J/s of useful energy?
3. HT An electric fire was left on for 30 minutes and the total energy transferred was 1.5kWh. What is the power rating of the fire?

# P3 Exam Practice Questions

**1** The students below are making statements about the use of alternative energy.

**Chevelle**
There are only a few locations for hydroelectric power stations.

**Ozair**
Wind turbines aren't reliable as it isn't always windy.

**Joseph**
Fossil fuels shouldn't be used as they generate greenhouse gases.

**Chloe**
Nuclear power stations have to be built near to water.

**(a)** Which student is giving an opinion? Put a tick (✓) in the box next to the correct name. **[1]**

Chevelle ☐    Ozair ☐    Joseph ☐    Chloe ☐

**(b)** Which **two** students are giving an explanation? Put ticks (✓) in the boxes next to the two correct names. **[1]**

Chevelle ☐    Ozair ☐    Joseph ☐    Chloe ☐

**2** Why is electricity described as a secondary energy source? **[1]**

**3** The diagram shows how electricity is generated in a fossil fuel power station.

Cold water

Furnace (fossil fuels)

Electricity to National Grid

**(a)** Explain how the generator produces electricity. **[2]**

**(b)** Why does the transformer step up the voltage to a high value in the overhead cables? **[1]**

**(c)** Explain how the turbine blades are driven. **[1]**

**4** What is the purpose of a Sankey diagram? **[2]**

**5** It's claimed that a modern 2.5MW wind turbine will, at a reasonable site, generate enough electricity each year to meet the annual needs of over 1400 households.

(a) (i) What is meant by a 'reasonable site'? [2]

...............................................................................................................................

...............................................................................................................................

(ii) Give one assumption that might have been made to make this statement. [1]

...............................................................................................................................

(b) What useful energy change occurs in a wind turbine? [1]

...............................................................................................................................

**6** Complete the table about the efficiency of the electrical appliances. [3]

| Electrical Appliance | Energy In | Useful Energy Out | Efficiency |
|---|---|---|---|
| Iron | 2000 joules/s | Heat: 1600 joules/s | |
| Radio | 200 joules/s | Sound: 60 joules/s | |
| Computer | 400 joules/s | Light: 180 joules/s Sound: 80 joules/s | |

**HT 7** This question examines the problems of supplying the UK with energy.

With the available gas supplies from the North Sea decreasing, the UK is relying increasingly more on imported gas. Many nuclear reactors are nearing the end of their useful lives and need replacing.

Explain why it **wouldn't** be a good idea for the UK to replace nuclear power stations with gas power stations. What are the advantages of building new nuclear power stations to replace the old ones? [6]

🖉 *The quality of written communication will be assessed in your answer to this question.*

...............................................................................................................................

...............................................................................................................................

...............................................................................................................................

...............................................................................................................................

...............................................................................................................................

...............................................................................................................................

...............................................................................................................................

# P4 Explaining Motion

## Velocity

**Velocity** tells you an object's...
- speed
- direction of travel.

(HT) For example, if a lorry travels along a straight road at 15m/s (metres per second), in one direction, the velocity is +15m/s. If it then travels in the opposite direction at the same speed, the velocity is -15m/s.

It doesn't matter which direction is called **positive** or **negative** as long as opposite directions have opposite signs.

This idea is also used when describing **distance**:
- Changes in distance in one direction are described as positive.
- In the opposite direction they're negative.

## Calculating Speed

To calculate an object's speed you need to know...
- the **distance** it has travelled
- the **time** it took to travel that distance.

You can calculate speed using this formula:

$$\text{Speed (m/s)} = \frac{\text{Distance travelled (m)}}{\text{Time taken (s)}} \qquad \frac{d}{s \times t}$$

The formula calculates an **average speed** over the total distance travelled, even if the speed of an object isn't constant.

The speed of an object at a particular point in time is called the **instantaneous speed**.

### Example

A car travels 10 metres in five seconds. What is its average speed?

$$\text{Speed} = \frac{\text{Distance travelled}}{\text{Time taken}} = \frac{10\text{m}}{5\text{s}} = \textbf{2m/s}$$

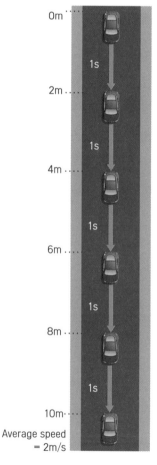

Average speed = 2m/s

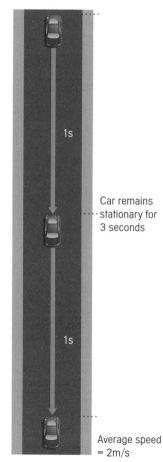

Car remains stationary for 3 seconds

Average speed = 2m/s

## Distance–Time Graphs

The slope, or **gradient**, of a **distance–time graph** is a measure of the **speed** of the object. The **steeper the slope**, the **greater the speed**.

The graph shows the following:

**①** A stationary person standing 15m away from point O.

**②** A person moving at a constant speed.

**③** A person moving at a greater constant speed.

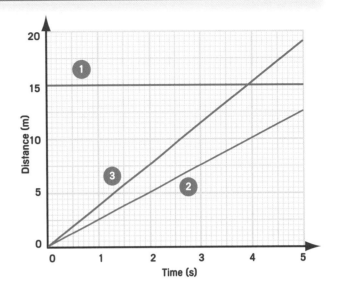

## HT Displacement–Time Graphs

You can calculate the speed of an object by working out the gradient of a displacement–time graph:

**①** Take any two points on the gradient.

**②** Read off the displacement travelled between these points.

**③** Note the time taken between these points.

**④** Divide the displacement by the time.

For example:

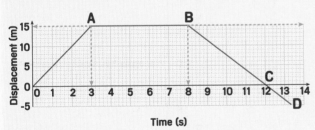

Speed from O to A = $\dfrac{15\text{m}}{3\text{s}}$ = **5m/s**

Speed from A to B = $\dfrac{15\text{m} - 15\text{m}}{5\text{s}}$ = **0m/s**

Speed from B to C = $\dfrac{15\text{m}}{4\text{s}}$ = **3.75m/s**

Speed from C to D = **3.75m/s**

So, the object…

- travelled at 5m/s for three seconds
- remained stationary for five seconds
- travelled at 3.75m/s for four seconds back to the starting point
- continued with a negative speed to point D. The displacement is now negative.

Remember…

- this calculation only works when looking at straight line sections
- when the object reaches point C, the average velocity for the journey is O because it's back where it started
- if you're asked to give velocity you need to indicate the direction. If the velocity in the first section is positive, the velocity in the last section will be negative because the object is moving in the opposite direction
- the displacement of an object at a given moment is its net distance from its starting point together with an indication of direction. So, the displacement at C is O
- the gradient of a displacement–time graph is the velocity (the velocity is negative between points B and D because the gradient is negative).

# P4 Explaining Motion

## Curvy Distance–Time Graphs

The **instantaneous velocity** of an object is its instantaneous speed together with an indication of direction.

**HT** When the line of a **distance–time graph** is curved, it means the **speed** of an object is **changing**:

- 0 to A – the line is curved. The object must be speeding up because the gradient is increasing.
- A to B – the line curves the other way. The object must be slowing down because the gradient is decreasing.

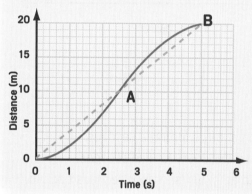

Because the graph is curved it's difficult to work out the **instantaneous speed**, but you can work out the average speed by dividing the total distance by the total time.

$$\text{Speed} = \frac{\text{Distance}}{\text{Time}}$$

$$= \frac{20\text{m}}{5\text{s}}$$

$$= 4\text{m/s}$$

The dashed line shows the average speed. Where the gradient is…

- **steeper** than the dashed line, the object is travelling **faster** than the average speed
- **less steep** than the dashed line, the object is travelling **slower** than the average speed.

## Speed–Time Graphs

The slope, or **gradient**, of a speed–time graph represents how quickly an object is increasing in speed (i.e. **accelerating**). The steeper the slope, the faster its speed is increasing.

Speed–time graphs are used in **lorry tachographs** to make sure that drivers…

- don't exceed the speed limit
- rest for suitable amounts of time.

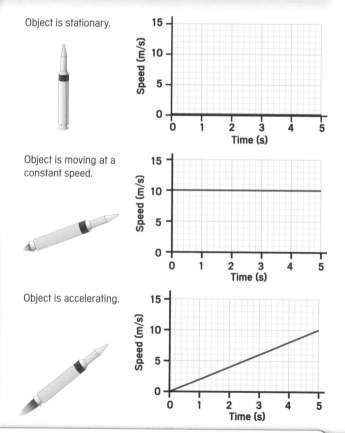

Object is stationary.

Object is moving at a constant speed.

Object is accelerating.

### Quick Test

1. A student plots a speed–time graph. The graph gives a horizontal straight line. What does that tell you about the acceleration?
2. **HT** A man walks North at 2m/s for 10 seconds, then rests for another 20s. What is his displacement?

## HT Understanding Velocity–Time Graphs

The quantity **velocity** has both **speed** and **direction**. A change in either (or both) the speed or direction of travel will cause a change in velocity. A velocity–time graph can have negative values for the velocity axis.

Look at the first velocity–time graph shown opposite:

- Car A is at rest.
- Car B is travelling with a constant velocity of 18m/s.
- Car C has a constantly increasing velocity (accelerating).
- Car D has a velocity that is decreasing at a constant rate (decelerating).

The second velocity–time graph shows a ball travelling at a constant speed of 10m/s, in one direction, for two seconds. It has an elastic collision with a wall before rebounding in the opposite direction at the same speed. Notice that the velocity will have changed because the direction of travel has changed. The speed remains constant at 10m/s.

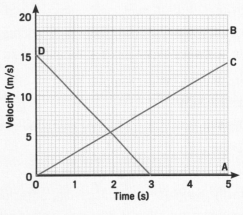

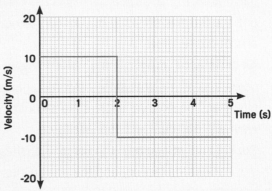

## Calculating Acceleration

Acceleration, change in speed and time are related by this formula:

Acceleration (m/s²) = $\dfrac{\text{Change in speed (m/s)}}{\text{Time taken (s)}}$

$\dfrac{v}{a \times t}$

where $v$ is change in speed, $a$ is acceleration and $t$ is time taken

### Example

A car is travelling at 2m/s when the driver accelerates to 10m/s in four seconds. What is the acceleration?

$$\text{Acceleration} = \frac{\text{Change in speed}}{\text{Time taken}}$$

$$\text{Acceleration} = \frac{10 - 2}{4}$$

$$= \frac{8}{4}$$

$$= 2\text{m/s}^2$$

### HT Example

The graph shows the motion of a car accelerating from rest. Use the graph to calculate the car's acceleration.

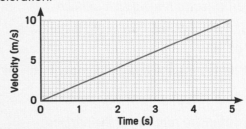

The gradient of a velocity–time graph can be used to find the acceleration.

$$\underset{\text{(acceleration, m/s}^2\text{)}}{\text{Gradient}} = \frac{\text{Change in velocity (m/s)}}{\text{Time taken (s)}}$$

$$= \frac{10 - 0\text{m/s}}{5\text{s}}$$

$$= 2\text{m/s}^2$$

# P4 Explaining Motion

## Forces

A **force** occurs when two objects **interact** with each other. Whenever one object exerts a force on another, it always experiences a force in return.

The forces in an **interaction pair** are...

- **equal** in size
- **opposite** in direction and they act on different objects.

Here are some examples of forces in action:

- **Gravity (weight)** – two masses are attracted to each other, e.g. you are attracted to the Earth and the Earth is attracted to you with an equal and opposite force.
- **Air resistance (drag)** – the air tries to slow down a skydiver by pushing upwards against him/her. The skydiver pushes the air out of the way with an equal and opposite force.
- **Rocket and jet engines** – the engine pushes gas backwards (action) and the gas pushes the rocket forwards (reaction).

(HT) A person moves by applying a force to the ground (they push on the ground). There will be an equal and opposite force generated (the ground pushes back on the person). The person moves because they have a much smaller mass than the Earth.

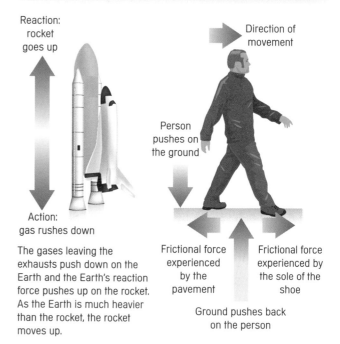

Reaction: rocket goes up

Action: gas rushes down

Direction of movement

Person pushes on the ground

Frictional force experienced by the pavement

Frictional force experienced by the sole of the shoe

Ground pushes back on the person

The gases leaving the exhausts push down on the Earth and the Earth's reaction force pushes up on the rocket. As the Earth is much heavier than the rocket, the rocket moves up.

## Friction and Reaction

Some forces only occur as a response to another force.

When an object is resting on a surface...

- the object is pulled down onto the surface by gravity
- the surface pushes up on the object with an equal force.

This is called the **reaction of the surface**.

When two objects try to slide past one another, both objects experience a force that tries to **stop them moving**. This is called **friction**.

Objects don't have to be moving to experience friction. For example, the friction from a car's brakes stops it rolling down a hill.

Friction and the reaction of a surface arise in response to the action of an applied force, and their size matches the applied force up to a limit.

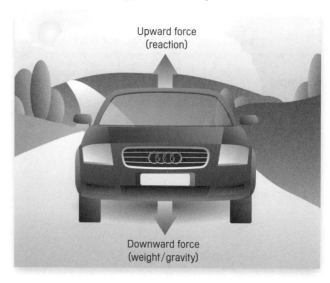

Upward force (reaction)

Downward force (weight/gravity)

**Force • Gravity • Friction**

## Forces and Motion

Arrows are used when drawing diagrams of **forces**:
- The size of the arrow represents the size of the force.
- The direction of the arrow shows the direction the force is acting in.

*N.B. Force arrows are always drawn with the tail of the arrow touching the object even if the force is pushing the object.*

If more than one force acts on an object they will...
- add up if they are acting in the same direction
- subtract if they are acting in opposite directions.

The overall effect of adding or subtracting these forces is called the **resultant force**.

Resultant force = ⟶ 3N

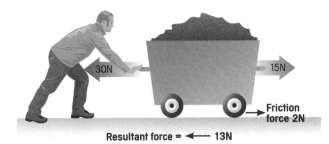

Resultant force = ⟵ 13N

## Momentum

**Momentum** is a measure of the motion of an object.

You can calculate the momentum of an object using this formula:

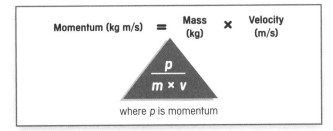

Momentum (kg m/s) **=** Mass (kg) **×** Velocity (m/s)

$$\frac{p}{m \times v}$$

where *p* is momentum

If a car and a lorry are travelling at the same speed, the lorry will have more momentum because it has a bigger mass.

### Example
A car has a mass of 1200kg and is travelling at a velocity of 30m/s. What is its momentum?

Momentum = Mass × Velocity
= 1200kg × 30m/s
= **36 000kg m/s**

# P4 Explaining Motion

## Change in Momentum

If the **resultant force** acting on an object is **zero**, its momentum will **not change**. So, if the object is...

- stationary, it will remain stationary
- already moving, it will continue moving in a straight line at a steady speed.

If the resultant force acting on an object is **not zero**, it causes a **change** of momentum in the direction of the force. This could...

- make a stationary object move
- increase or decrease an object's speed
- change an object's direction.

The extent of the change in momentum depends on...

- the size of the resultant force
- the length of time the force is acting on the object.

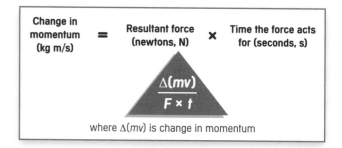

| Change in momentum (kg m/s) | = | Resultant force (newtons, N) | × | Time the force acts for (seconds, s) |

$$\frac{\Delta(mv)}{F \times t}$$

where $\Delta(mv)$ is change in momentum

## Collisions

**Collisions** can cause changes in an object's momentum. For example, a car with a mass of 1000kg, travelling at 10m/s, has a momentum of 10 000kg m/s. If the car is involved in a collision and comes to a sudden stop, it would experience a change in momentum of 10 000kg m/s.

Sudden changes in momentum as a result of a collision can affect...

- the car
- the passengers – leading to injuries.

If the change in momentum is **spread** out over a longer period of time, the resultant force will be **smaller**.

## Safety Devices

The force of the **impact** on the human body can be reduced by increasing the **time** of the impact. This is the purpose of road safety devices, for example...

- seat belts
- crumple zones – crumple on impact (e.g. motorcycle and bicycle helmets)
- air bags.

Crumple zone

## Speeding Up and Slowing Down

Cars and bicycles have a...

- **driving force** produced by the engine (car) or the energy of the cyclist (bicycle)
- **counter force** caused by **friction** and air resistance.

If the driving force is...

- **bigger than** the counter force, the vehicle speeds up
- **equal to** the counter force, the vehicle travels at a constant speed in a straight line
- **smaller than** the counter force, the vehicle slows down.

**Car Speeds Up**

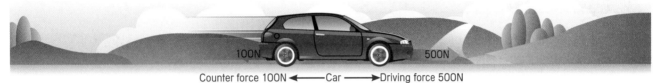

Counter force 100N ◄──── Car ────► Driving force 500N

**Car Travels at a Constant Speed**

Counter force 500N ◄──── Car ────► Driving force 500N

**Car Slows Down**

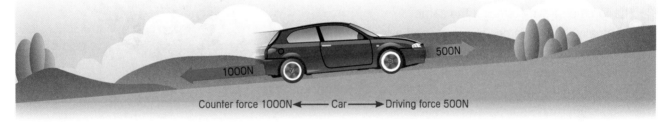

Counter force 1000N ◄──── Car ────► Driving force 500N

## Kinetic Energy

A moving object has **kinetic energy**.

The amount of kinetic energy an object has depends on its...

- **mass**
- **velocity**.

The greater the mass and velocity of an object, the more kinetic energy it has. You can calculate kinetic energy using this formula:

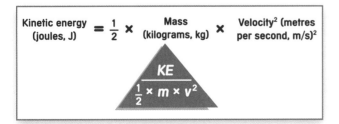

**Example**

A bicycle of mass 50kg is moving at a velocity of 8m/s. How much kinetic energy does it have?

$$\text{Kinetic energy} = \frac{1}{2} \times \text{Mass} \times \text{Velocity}^2$$
$$= \frac{1}{2} \times 50\text{kg} \times (8\text{m/s})^2$$
$$= \frac{1}{2} \times 50 \times 64$$
$$= \textbf{1600J}$$

# P4 Explaining Motion

## Objects Thrown Upwards

Consider a person throwing a ball up in the air. As the ball leaves the hand, an initial force is applied vertically upwards. There will be two forces opposing the motion:

- **Air resistance**
- **Gravity**.

As soon as the ball leaves the hand, these forces will cause the ball to lose speed. There is no upward force once the ball has left the hand.

## Objects Falling

Consider a skydiver jumping out of a plane. As the skydiver jumps out of the plane, only one force is acting in the vertical direction – the unbalanced force of **gravity**.

The skydiver will start to accelerate downwards:

1 As the skydiver falls, he/she will start to experience a new force of **air resistance**. The faster the skydiver falls, the greater this air resistance force becomes.

2 The force of gravity remains the same.

3 Eventually the two forces of gravity and air resistance become equal and opposite.

4 The skydiver now stops accelerating and travels at a constant speed.

## Work and Energy

Work is done by a force to move an object, resulting in the **transfer** of **energy**.

When work is done…

- **on** an object, the object **gains** energy
- **by** an object, the object **loses** energy.

The total amount of energy remains the same, i.e. energy is **conserved**.

| Amount of energy transferred (joules, J) = Work done (joules, J) |
|---|

When a force makes an object's velocity increase…

- work is done on the object by the force
- the object gains kinetic energy.

If you ignore drag and friction, the increase in kinetic energy will be **equal to** the work done by the force. But, in reality, some of the energy will be dissipated (lost) as heat.

The relationship between work done, force and distance is shown by this formula:

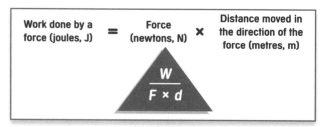

| Work done by a force (joules, J) | = | Force (newtons, N) | X | Distance moved in the direction of the force (metres, m) |

$$\frac{W}{F \times d}$$

Air resistance or friction will cause the gain in an object's kinetic energy to be less than the work done on it by an applied force in the direction of motion because some energy is dissipated through heating.

**Key Words**          **Air resistance • Gravity**

## Gravitational Potential Energy

When an object is lifted above the ground...
- work is done by the lifting force against gravity
- the object has the potential to do work when it falls, e.g. a diver standing on a diving board.

This is called **gravitational potential energy** (**GPE**).

You can calculate change in GPE using this formula:

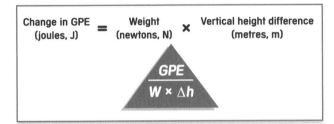

$$\frac{GPE}{W \times \Delta h}$$

*N.B. To find the GPE, you use weight not mass.*

If an object is dropped, its GPE decreases and converts into kinetic energy.

### Example

An object is dropped from a height of 5m. It has a mass of 2kg and weighs 20N. How much kinetic energy does it gain?

Change in GPE = Weight × Vertical height difference
$$= 20N \times 5m$$
$$= \mathbf{100J}$$

The object...
- loses 100J of gravitational potential energy
- gains 100J of kinetic energy.

(HT) You can use the kinetic energy formula to work out the velocity of a falling object. In the example above we know that the object has gained 100J of kinetic energy.

$$\text{Kinetic energy} = \tfrac{1}{2} \times \text{Mass} \times \text{Velocity}^2$$
$$100 = \tfrac{1}{2} \times 2 \times v^2$$
$$100 = v^2$$
$$v = \sqrt{100}$$
$$= \mathbf{10m/s}$$

## Quick Test

1. With a rocket, the engine pushes gas backwards. What is the name of that force?
2. A force of 12N acts on a truck for two seconds. What is the change in momentum?
3. Give three examples of safety devices used in cars.
4. A cyclist of mass 60kg is moving at a speed of 4m/s. How much kinetic energy does the cyclist have?
5. (HT) A person weighing 800N gains 16 000J of gravitational potential energy as they're carried up in a lift. How high did they go?
6. (HT) A person has 800J of kinetic energy. If they have a mass of 100kg, how fast are they travelling?

# P4 Exam Practice Questions

**1 (a)** The graph shows three different journeys. Match statements **A**, **B** and **C** with the labels **1–3** on the graph.

**A**   The person is moving at the fastest speed.   ◯

**B**   The person is moving at the slowest speed.   ◯

**C**   The person is stationary.   ◯

[2]

**(b)** What does the gradient of a distance–time graph tell you?   [1]

..............................................................................................................................................................

**2 (a)** A car is measured travelling 40 metres in 5 seconds. How fast is the car travelling? Put a (ring) around the correct answer.   [1]

   **200m/s**     **8m**     **20m/s**     **8m/s**     **200m**

**(b)** A motorcycle accelerates from rest and reaches a speed of 30m/s in 4 seconds. What is the acceleration of the motorcycle? Put a (ring) around the correct answer.   [1]

   **120m/s²**     **7.5m/s**     **120m/s**     **34m/s**     **7.5m/s²**

**3** Which of the following statements are correct? Put ticks (✓) in the boxes next to the **two** correct statements.   [2]

Speed–time graphs are used in lorry tachographs to make sure drivers rest for the appropriate time.   ◯

Friction is a force that always opposes motion.   ◯

The instantaneous speed is the maximum speed reached during a journey.   ◯

The gradient of a distance–time graph is the acceleration.   ◯

**4** A person starts to walk in a straight line along a flat pavement. Explain what forces are involved in the process of walking.   [6]

🖉 *The quality of written communication will be assessed in your answer to this question.*

..............................................................................................................................................................

..............................................................................................................................................................

..............................................................................................................................................................

..............................................................................................................................................................

..............................................................................................................................................................

..............................................................................................................................................................

..............................................................................................................................................................

**5** A car of mass 1500kg is travelling along a road at a velocity of 45m/s.

(a) What is the momentum of the car? [2]

(b) What is the acceleration if the speed increases from 45m/s to 55m/s in 4 seconds? [2]

**6** Which of the following statements are correct? Put ticks (✓) in the boxes next to the **two** correct statements. [2]

The change in momentum depends on the size of the force acting and the time it acts for. ☐

For an object moving in a straight line, if the driving force is larger than friction, the object will slow down. ☐

If the resultant force on a car is zero, its momentum is constant. ☐

The energy of a moving object is called work. ☐

**HT 7** A ball of weight 40N is dropped from a height of 20 metres. Calculate the velocity of the ball just before it hits the ground. Take the mass of the ball to be 4kg. [2]

**8** A 150kg dodgem car travelling at 3m/s collides with a rubber wall in the fairground and rebounds with a speed of 2m/s.

(a) What is the change in momentum? [2]

(b) If the collision lasted for 0.5 seconds, what force acted on the dodgem car? [2]

(c) Why did the driver bend his knees during the impact? [1]

# P5 Electric Circuits

## Static Electricity

When you rub two objects together, they become **electrically charged** as **electrons** (which are negatively charged) are transferred from one object to the other:

- The object **receiving** the electrons becomes **negatively** charged.
- The object **giving up** electrons becomes **positively** charged.

The electrical charge is called **static electricity**.

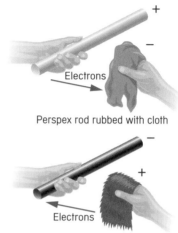

Perspex rod rubbed with cloth

Ebonite rod rubbed with fur

## Repulsion and Attraction

When two charged materials are brought together, they exert a **force** on each other:

- Two materials with the same type of charge **repel** each other.
- Two materials with different charges **attract** each other.

For example, if you move...

- a positively charged Perspex rod near to another positively charged Perspex rod suspended on a string, the suspended rod will be **repelled**
- a negatively charged ebonite rod near to a positively charged suspended Perspex rod, the suspended Perspex rod will be **attracted**.

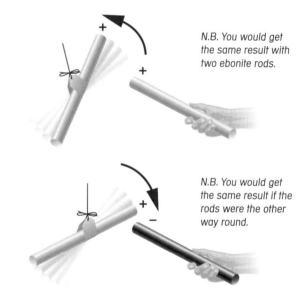

*N.B. You would get the same result with two ebonite rods.*

*N.B. You would get the same result if the rods were the other way round.*

## Electric Currents

An **electric current** is a **flow of charge**. It's measured in **amperes** (amps).

In an electric circuit...

- the components and wires are full of charges that are free to move
- the battery causes the free charges to move
- the charges aren't used up but flow in a continuous loop.

In **metal conductors** there are lots of charges free to move, but in **insulators** there are no charges free to move.

Metals contain **free electrons** in their structure, which move to create an **electric current**.

**Key Words**      Electron • Static electricity • Force • Current

## Circuit Symbols

Standard symbols are used to represent components in circuits.

| Cell | ⊣⊢ | Fixed resistor | ▭ |
|---|---|---|---|
| Power supply (battery) | ⊣⊢⋯⊣⊢ | Variable resistor | (symbol) |
| Filament lamp | ⊗ | Thermistor | (symbol) |
| Switch (open) (closed) | (symbol) | Voltmeter | Ⓥ |
| Light dependent resistor (LDR) | (symbol) | Ammeter | Ⓐ |

## Types of Current

A **direct current** (d.c.) always flows in the same direction. Cells and batteries supply direct current.

An **alternating current** (a.c.) changes the direction of flow back and forth continuously and is used for mains electricity. The mains supply of **voltage** to your home is 230 volts.

**HT** Alternating current is used for mains supply instead of direct current. This is because…
- it's easier to generate
- it can be distributed more efficiently
- only alternating current can be used in a transformer.

## Potential Difference and Current

**Potential difference** is another name for **voltage**:
- The potential difference between two points in the circuit is the **work done** on (or by) a given amount of charge as it moves between these points.
- It's measured in **volts** (V) using a **voltmeter** connected in parallel across the component.

A bulb with 3 volts across it is taking 3 joules of energy from every unit of charge. This energy is given off as heat and light.

The greater the potential difference across a component, the greater the current will be.

When you add more batteries in series, the potential difference and the current increase.

**HT** When you add more batteries in parallel…
- the total potential difference and current remain the same
- each battery supplies less current.

**Increasing the Potential Difference Makes the Bulb Brighter**

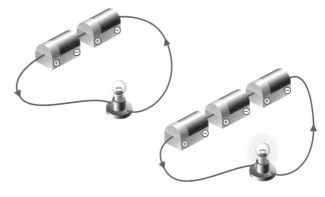

# P5 Electric Circuits

## Resistance and Current

Components **resist** the flow of **charge** through them. Examples of components are...

- resistors
- lamps
- motors.

The connecting wires in the circuit have some **resistance**, but it's so small that it's usually ignored.

The **greater the resistance** in a circuit, the **smaller the current** will be.

Two lamps together in a circuit with one cell have a certain resistance. If you include another cell in the circuit, it provides...

- a greater **potential difference**
- a greater **current**.

When you add resistors in **series**, the battery has to push charges through more resistors, so the **resistance increases**.

When you add resistors in **parallel**, there are more paths for the charges to flow along, so the total **resistance reduces** and the total **current increases**.

When an electric current flows through a component, it causes the component to heat up. This heating effect is large enough to make a lamp filament glow.

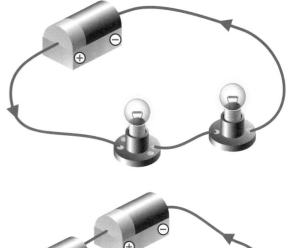

The second circuit has more batteries and so has a higher voltage. This causes a greater current to flow than in the first circuit.

(HT) As the current flows...

- moving charges collide with the vibrating **ions** in the wire, giving them energy
- the increase in energy causes the component to heat up.

## Calculating Resistance

You can calculate resistance using this formula:

$$\text{Resistance (ohms, } \Omega\text{)} = \frac{\text{Voltage (volts, V)}}{\text{Current (amperes, A)}}$$

where *I* is current

$$\frac{V}{I \times R}$$

**Example**

A circuit has a current of 3 amps and a voltage of 6V. What is the resistance?

$$\text{Resistance} = \frac{\text{Voltage}}{\text{Current}} = \frac{6V}{3A} = 2\Omega$$

(HT) You can work out the potential difference or current by rearranging the resistance formula.

**Example**

A circuit has a current of 0.2 amps and a bulb with a resistance of 15 ohms. What is the reading on the voltmeter?

Potential difference = Current × Resistance

= 0.2A × 15Ω

= **3V**

## Current–Voltage Graphs

As long as a component's resistance stays constant, the current through the resistor is **directly proportional** to the **voltage** across the resistor. This is regardless of which direction the current is flowing.

This means that a graph showing current through the component, and voltage across the component, will be a **straight line** through 0.

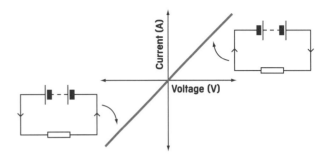

## Thermistors and LDRs

The resistance of a **thermistor** depends on its temperature. As the temperature increases…

- its resistance decreases
- more current flows.

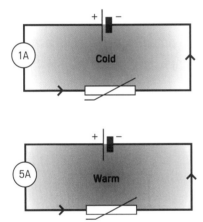

The resistance of a **light dependent resistor** (**LDR**) depends on light intensity. As the amount of light falling on it increases…

- its resistance decreases
- more current flows.

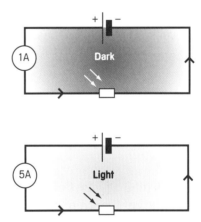

## Quick Test

1. If a Perspex rod is rubbed with a cloth, it loses electrons. What charge will the rod now have?
2. What is the circuit symbol for a light dependent resistor?
3. If a battery of 12V is connected across a bulb and a current of 3A flows through it, what is the resistance of the bulb?
4. How could the relationship between the current and voltage across a component be described if the resistance is constant?
5. HT A 12V battery is connected across a resistor of resistance 24Ω. What current flows?
6. HT Why does a component heat up when a current flows?

# P5 Electric Circuits

## Series Circuits

When two components are connected in series to a battery...

- the **current** flowing through each component is the same, i.e. $A_1 = A_2 = A_3$
- the **potential difference** across the components adds up to the potential difference across the battery, i.e. $V_1 = V_2 + V_3$
- the potential difference is largest across components with the greatest **resistance**.

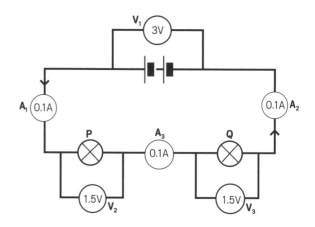

**HT** The above also applies when **more than two** components are connected in series to a battery.

As shown above right, the voltmeter should be connected in parallel across a component to measure the potential difference between any two chosen points. The voltage across the battery (measured in volts, V) provides a measure of the 'push' of the battery on the charges in the circuit.

**HT** The work done on each unit of charge by the battery must equal the work done by it on the circuit components. More work is done by the charge moving through a large resistance than through a small one.

A change in the resistance of one component (variable resistor, LDR or thermistor) will result in a change in the potential differences across all the components.

## Parallel Circuits

In parallel circuits with one component per parallel path...

- the **current** flowing through each component depends on the **resistance** of each component
- the total current running from (and back to) the battery is equal to the sum of the current through each of the parallel components, i.e. $A_1 = A_2 + A_3 = A_4$
- the current is greatest through the component with the smallest resistance.

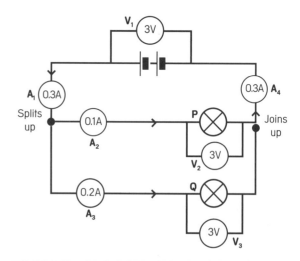

**HT** The current through each component is the same as if it were the only component present. If a second identical component is added in parallel...

- the same current flows through each component
- the total current through the battery increases.

**HT** The same **voltage** causes more current to flow through a smaller resistance than a bigger one.

The **potential difference** across each component is equal to the potential difference of the battery.

## Electromagnetic Induction

When you move a magnet into a coil of wire, a **voltage** is induced between the ends of the wire because the **magnetic field** is being cut.

If the ends of the coil are connected to make a complete circuit, a **current** will be induced.

This is called **electromagnetic induction**.

Moving the magnet into the coil induces a current in one direction. You can then induce a current in the opposite direction by...

- moving the magnet out of the coil
- moving the other pole of the magnet into the coil.

If there's no movement of the coil or magnet, there's no induced current.

**Moving the Magnet into the Coil**

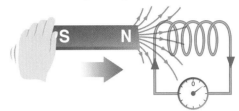

**Moving the Magnet out of the Coil**

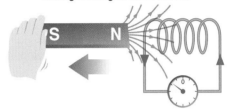

**Moving the Other Pole of the Magnet into the Coil**

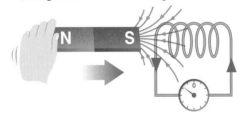

## The Electric Generator

Mains electricity is produced by **generators**. Generators use the principle of **electromagnetic induction** to generate electricity by rotating a magnet inside a coil.

The size of the induced voltage can be increased by...

- increasing the speed of rotation of the magnet
- increasing the strength of the magnetic field, possibly by using an electromagnet
- increasing the number of turns on the coil
- placing an iron core inside the coil.

HT As the magnet rotates, the **voltage** induced in the coil changes direction and size as shown in the diagram. The **current** that's produced is an **alternating current** as it reverses its direction of flow every half turn of the magnet. The direction of the voltage and current after one full turn of the magnet are in the same direction as they were at the start before the magnet was turned.

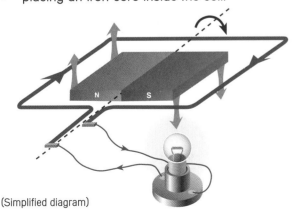

(Simplified diagram)

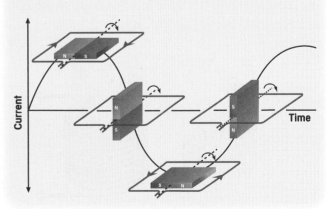

# P5 Electric Circuits

## Power

When electric charge flows through a component (or device), work is done by the power supply. **Energy is transferred** from the power supply to the component and/or its surroundings.

Power...
- is a measure of the rate of energy transfer to an appliance or device and/or its surroundings
- is measured in watts (W).

You can calculate power using the following formula:

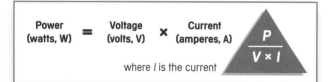

$$\text{Power (watts, W)} = \text{Voltage (volts, V)} \times \text{Current (amperes, A)}$$

where *I* is the current

$$\frac{P}{V \times I}$$

**Example**

An electric motor works at a current of 3A and a voltage of 24V. What is the power of the motor?

Power = Voltage × Current
= 24V × 3A
= **72W**

(HT) You can work out the potential difference or current by rearranging the power formula.

**Example**

A 4W light bulb works at a current of 2A. What is the potential difference?

$$\text{Potential difference} = \frac{\text{Power}}{\text{Current}} = \frac{4W}{2A} = \textbf{2V}$$

## Transformers

**Transformers** are used to change the **voltage** of an **alternating current**. They consist of two coils of wire, called the primary and secondary coils, wrapped around a soft iron core.

When two coils of wire are close to each other, a changing magnetic field in one coil caused by changes in the current can induce a voltage in the other:
- Alternating current flowing through the primary coil creates an alternating magnetic field.
- This changing field then induces an alternating current in the secondary coil.

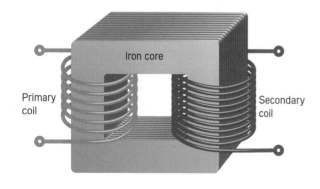

Primary coil
Iron core
Secondary coil

(HT) The amount by which a transformer changes the voltage depends on the number of turns on the primary and secondary coils. The changing current in the primary coil will cause a changing magnetic field in the iron core, which in turn will cause a changing potential difference across the secondary coil. You need to be able to use this equation:

| Voltage on primary coil ($V_p$) | | Number of turns on primary coil, $N_p$ |
|:---:|:---:|:---:|
| Voltage on secondary coil ($V_s$) | = | Number of turns on secondary coil, $N_s$ |

**Example**

A transformer has 1000 turns on the primary coil and 200 turns on the secondary coil. If a voltage of 250V is applied to the primary coil, what is the voltage across the secondary coil?

$$\frac{250}{V_s} = \frac{1000}{200}$$

$$250 = 5V_s \text{ so } V_s = \frac{250}{5} = \textbf{50V}$$

Transformer • Alternating current

## Electric Motors

An electric motor consists of a coil of wire that rotates in between the opposite poles of a permanent magnet, when a current flows through the coil.

A current-carrying wire (or coil)…

- can exert a force on a permanent magnet or another current-carrying wire nearby
- **experiences a force** if placed in a **magnetic field** whose lines of force are at right angles to the wire. The force will be at right angles to **both** the current direction and the lines of force of the **magnetic field**. If the current in a wire travels parallel to the magnetic **field lines**, it doesn't experience a force.

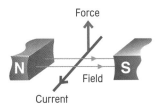

When a current flows through the coil, it will cut the field lines in opposite directions on each side of the coil. This creates a pair of forces in opposite directions and causes the coil to rotate around its axis.

A **commutator** is a rotary switch that turns with the coil, but the brushes that touch it remain fixed. This has the effect of making sure that, as the coil rotates, the current direction into the coil is switched.

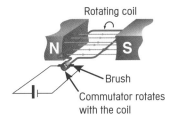

The current always cuts the **field lines** nearest the South pole of the fixed magnet in the same direction, no matter how many times the coil spins.

Similarly, the current will always cut the field lines nearest the North pole in the opposite direction. This produces a pair of opposing forces whose directions remain the same, giving continuous rotation.

## Uses of Electric Motors

Electric motors have a role and use in many devices:

| Device | How the Motor is Used |
|---|---|
| Hard disk drive | To rotate the hard disk at high speed under the read / write heads. |
| DVD player | To rotate the disk so that the information can be read. |
| Electric motor vehicle | To provide traction via the transmission to the rear wheels. |
| Washing machine | To rotate the drum and agitate the wash so that all the clothes are washed effectively. |
| Tumble dryer | To rotate the drum and provide uniform heat to all the items being dried. |
| Microwave oven | To rotate the food and make sure that it's evenly heated. |

## Quick Test

1. What principle do generators use to generate electricity?
2. What is the power of a 12V lamp in a circuit where a 0.5A current flows?
3. In a transformer, what induces a voltage across the secondary coil?
4. HT A transformer has a primary coil of 200 turns. If the transformer changes 12V to 240V, how many turns must be on the secondary coil?
5. HT A 60W light bulb has a 240V power supply connected across it. What current flows?

**1** Toni has suspended a positively charged Perspex rod on an insulated plastic thread. What will happen if she brings a negatively charged ebonite rod close to the Perspex rod? **[1]**

...................................................................................................................................................................

**2** Put a (ring) around the correct symbol for a cell. **[1]**

**3** Here is a table of data from an electrical experiment to find the resistance of three components. Complete the table by filling in the missing values.

| Component | Voltage (V) | Current (A) | Resistance (Ω) |
|---|---|---|---|
| Lamp | 8 | | 4 |
| Resistor | | 6 | 5 |
| Coil | 24 | 4 | |

**[3]**

**4** Give two ways to increase the size of an induced voltage in a generator. **[2]**

1. ...................................................................................................................................................

2. ...................................................................................................................................................

**5** Chevelle was experimenting by moving a magnet into a coil of wire that was connected to an ammeter. She noticed that the ammeter showed a current flowing in one direction. Four students are discussing how she could reverse the direction of the current.

**Jessie**
I would move the magnet into the coil more quickly.

**Sonny**
Try using a coil with more turns on it.

**Jake**
You could move the magnet out of the coil.

**Shanika**
Just rotate the magnet through 180° then move it out of the coil.

**(a)** Which student gave the correct way to reverse the current? Put a tick (✓) in the box next to the correct name. **[1]**

Jessie ◯    Sonny ◯    Jake ◯    Shanika ◯

**(b)** Which **two** students gave a way to increase the current? Put ticks (✓) in the boxes next to the two correct names. **[1]**

Jessie ◯    Sonny ◯    Jake ◯    Shanika ◯

**6** Imran used the following circuit to carry out an experiment to find out what was in the mystery box. He measured the current and calculated the resistance for a range of temperatures. His results are shown in the table.

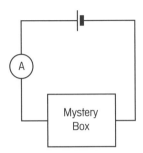

| Temperature (°C) | 100 | 80 | 60 | 40 | 20 | 0 |
|---|---|---|---|---|---|---|
| Resistance (Ω) | 50 | 62.5 | 83.3 | 125 | 250 | 260 |

**(a) (i)** What component might have been in the box? .......................................................................... **[1]**

  **(ii)** What conclusion can be drawn from the table about the relationship between resistance and temperature? **[1]**

....................................................................................................................................................

**(b)** The reading at 0°C doesn't fit the pattern. What mistake might Imran have made? **[1]**

....................................................................................................................................................

**(c)** How could the circuit be changed to act as a simple fire alarm? **[1]**

....................................................................................................................................................


**HT** **7** Explain how, when an alternating potential difference is applied across a primary coil of a transformer, it's possible to obtain an alternating potential difference of a higher value across the secondary coil. **[6]**
   ✎ *The quality of written communication will be assessed in your answer to this question.*

..........................................................................................................................................................

..........................................................................................................................................................

..........................................................................................................................................................

..........................................................................................................................................................

..........................................................................................................................................................

..........................................................................................................................................................

..........................................................................................................................................................

..........................................................................................................................................................

**8** A transformer has a primary coil of 3000 turns and is connected to a 150V alternating supply. If the output voltage is 900V, how many turns are there on the secondary coil? **[1]**

..........................................................................................................................................................

# P6 Radioactive Materials

## Atoms and Elements

All **elements** are made of **atoms**; each element contains only one type of atom. All atoms contain a **nucleus** and **electrons**.

The nucleus is made from **protons** and **neutrons**. Hydrogen (the lightest element) is the one exception; it has no neutrons, just one proton and one electron.

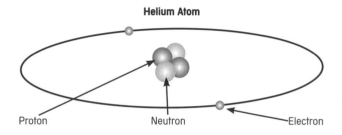

**Helium Atom**

Proton    Neutron    Electron

Radioactive elements emit ionising radiation all the time. Neither chemical reactions nor physical processes (e.g. smelting) can change the radioactive behaviour of a substance.

(HT) Every atom of a **particular element** always has the same number of protons. (If it contained a different number of protons, it would be a different element.) For example…
* hydrogen atoms have one proton
* helium atoms have two protons
* oxygen atoms have eight protons.

But some atoms of the same element can have **different numbers of neutrons** – these are isotopes. For example, there are three isotopes of oxygen:

Oxygen-16 has eight neutrons    Oxygen-17 has nine neutrons    Oxygen-18 has 10 neutrons.

*N.B. All three of these isotopes have eight protons.*

## Ionising Radiation

Radioactive materials can give out three types of ionising radiation:
* **Alpha**
* **Beta**
* **Gamma**.

Different radioactive materials will give out any one, or a combination, of these radiations.

The different types of radiation have different penetrating powers.

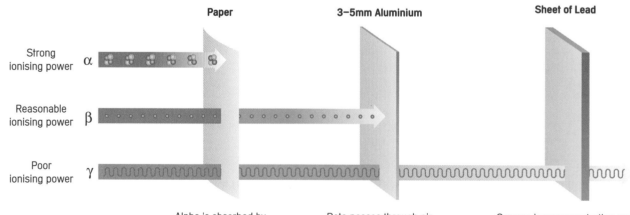

| | Paper | 3–5mm Aluminium | Sheet of Lead |
|---|---|---|---|

Strong ionising power α

Reasonable ionising power β

Poor ionising power γ

Alpha is absorbed by a few centimetres of air or a thin sheet of paper.

Beta passes through air and paper but is absorbed by a few millimetres of aluminium.

Gamma is very penetrating and needs many centimetres of lead or many metres of concrete to absorb most of it.

**Key Words** Element • Atom • Nucleus • Electron • Proton • Neutron • Isotope • Alpha • Beta • Gamma

## 🔒 Radioactive Decay

Ionising radiation is emitted when the nucleus of an unstable atom decays. The type of **radioactive decay** depends on why the nucleus is unstable; the process of decay helps the atom become more **stable**. During decay the number of protons may change. If this happens the element **changes** to another type.

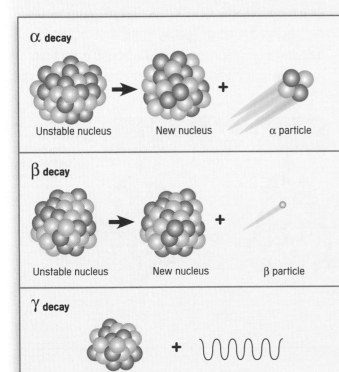

| | |
|---|---|
| **α decay**<br>Unstable nucleus → New nucleus + α particle | The original atom decays by ejecting an **alpha** (α) **particle** from the nucleus. This particle is a **helium nucleus**: a particle made of two protons and two neutrons. With **alpha decay** a new atom is formed. This new atom has two protons and two neutrons fewer than the original. |
| **β decay**<br>Unstable nucleus → New nucleus + β particle | The original atom decays by changing a neutron into a proton and an electron. This high energy electron, which is now ejected from the nucleus, is a **beta** (β) **particle**. With **beta decay** a new atom is formed. This new atom has one more proton and one less neutron than the original. |
| **γ decay**<br>Stable nucleus + γ radiation | After α or β decay, a nucleus sometimes contains surplus energy. It emits this as **gamma** (γ) radiation (very high frequency electromagnetic radiation). During gamma decay, only energy is emitted. This decay doesn't change the type of atom. |

## Background Radiation

Radioactive elements are found naturally in the environment and contribute to **background radiation**. If a person is irradiated, they're exposed to radiation. If they're **contaminated**, then radioactive material is on their skin, clothes or has entered their body.

Nothing can stop us being irradiated and contaminated by background radiation, but generally the levels are so low it's nothing to worry about. However, there appears to be a **correlation** between certain cancers and living in particular areas, especially among people who have lived in granite buildings for many years.

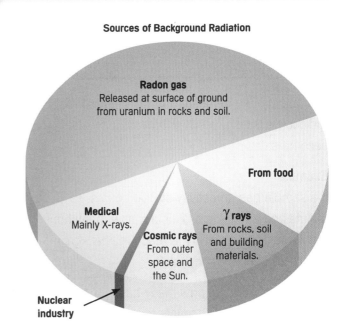

**Sources of Background Radiation**

Radon gas
Released at surface of ground from uranium in rocks and soil.

From food

Medical
Mainly X-rays.

Cosmic rays
From outer space and the Sun.

γ rays
From rocks, soil and building materials.

Nuclear industry

# P6 Radioactive Materials

## Measuring the Half-life

As a radioactive atom decays, its activity drops. This means that its radioactivity decreases over time.

The **half-life** of a substance is the time it takes for its radioactivity to halve.

Different substances have different half-lives, ranging from a few seconds to thousands of years.

Experiments to measure the half-life of radioactive elements need to be **repeated** several times and the activity levels for each experiment averaged to give more **reliable** data. Whilst half the number of radioactive atoms will decay in the time called the half-life, there might be slight variations each time the activity is measured.

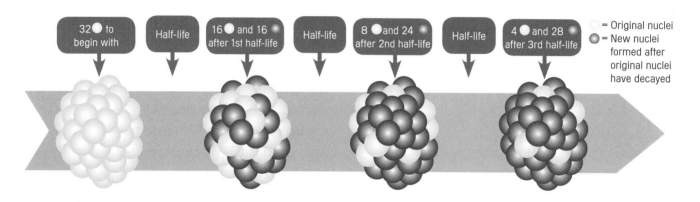

32 ○ to begin with — Half-life — 16 ○ and 16 ● after 1st half-life — Half-life — 8 ○ and 24 ● after 2nd half-life — Half-life — 4 ○ and 28 ● after 3rd half-life

○ = Original nuclei
● = New nuclei formed after original nuclei have decayed

## Half-life and Safety

A substance is considered safe once its activity drops to the same level as background radiation. This is a dose of around 3 **millisieverts** per year or 25 counts per minute with a standard detector.

Some substances decay quickly and could be safe in a very short time. Those with a long half-life remain harmful for thousands of years.

## HT Half-life Calculations

The half-life can be used to calculate how old a radioactive substance is, or how long it will take to become safe.

**Example**

If a sample has an activity of 800 counts per minute and a half-life of 2 hours, how many hours will it take for the activity to reach the background rate of 25 counts per minute?

We need to work out how many half-lives it takes for the sample of 800 counts to reach 25 counts.

**1** $\frac{800}{2} = 400$  **2** $\frac{400}{2} = 200$  **3** $\frac{200}{2} = 100$  **4** $\frac{100}{2} = 50$  **5** $\frac{50}{2} = 25$

It takes 5 half-lives to reach a count of 25, and each half-life takes 2 hours.

So, it takes 5 × 2 hours = **10 hours**

## Dangers of Radiation

Ionising radiation can break molecules into ions. These ions can damage living cells and the cells may be killed or become cancerous.

**(HT)** Ions are **very reactive** and can take part in other chemical reactions.

Many jobs involve using radioactive materials (e.g. workers in nuclear power stations, radiographers, etc.). People can become **irradiated** or **contaminated**, so their exposure needs to be carefully monitored.

Different types of radiation carry different risks:
- **Alpha** is the most dangerous if the source is **inside the body**; all the radiation will be absorbed by cells in the body.
- **Beta** is the most dangerous if the source is **outside the body**. Unlike alpha, it can penetrate the outer layer of skin and damage internal organs.
- **Gamma** can cause harm if it's absorbed by the cells, but it is weakly ionising and can pass straight through the body causing no damage at all.

The **sievert** is a measure of a radiation dose's potential to harm a person. It's based on both the type and the amount of radiation absorbed.

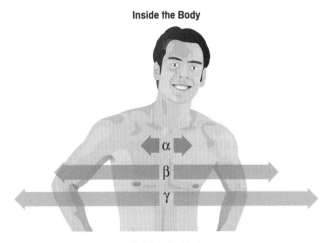

**Inside the Body**

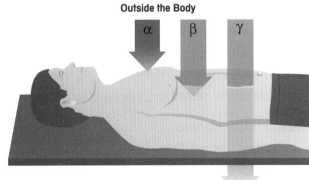

**Outside the Body**

## Uses of Radiation

Although using ionising radiation can be dangerous, there are many beneficial uses.

High-energy gamma rays in **cancer treatment** can destroy cancer cells but can damage healthy cells too. The radiation has to be carefully targeted from different angles to minimise the damage. Doctors need to carefully weigh the **risks** against the benefits before going ahead.

Radiation is also used in the following ways:
- To **sterilise surgical instruments** and to **sterilise food**. This kills bacteria.
- As a tracer in the body, for example in **PET (Positron Emission Tomography)** scans.

**(HT)** In PET scans, radio-labelled glucose is injected into the patient's bloodstream, from which it is absorbed into the tissues, as glucose is needed for respiration. A pair of gamma ray photons is emitted from the radio-labelled glucose in active cells. These are detected by gamma ray cameras and used to produce an image, for instance of the brain, showing any abnormal regions. Cancerous cells often absorb more glucose, so they will emit more gamma rays than surrounding tissues and will be detected.

In radiotherapy, a beam of gamma rays is focused from different angles onto cancer cells to destroy them. This gives a concentrated dose to the cancer cells but a smaller dose to the surrounding tissue.

**Key Words** | Alpha • Beta • Gamma • Risk |

## Nuclear Waste

Nuclear power stations release energy due to changes in the **nucleus** of radioactive substances. They don't produce carbon dioxide but they do produce radioactive waste.

**Nuclear waste** is categorised into three types:

- **High-level waste** (HLW) – very radioactive waste that has to be stored carefully. Fortunately, only small amounts are produced and it doesn't remain radioactive for long, so it's put into short-term storage.
- **Intermediate-level waste** (ILW) – not as radioactive as HLW but it remains radioactive for thousands of years. Increasing amounts are produced; deciding how to store it is a problem. At the moment most ILW is mixed with concrete and stored in big containers, but this isn't a permanent solution.
- **Low-level waste** (LLW) – only slightly radioactive waste that is sealed and placed in landfills.

Nuclear power stations…

- don't emit smoke from chimneys as happens in fossil-fuel power stations
- don't release greenhouse gases into the atmosphere.

Spent fuel rods from the reactors in nuclear power stations…

- still contain 90% uranium
- are sent away to be reprocessed and used to make new fuel rods
- are examples of high-level waste.

If you were standing within a few metres of unprotected spent fuel rods, you would receive a lethal dose of radiation in a few seconds.

This table shows risks related to radiation dose:

| Situation | Dose (millisieverts) | Risk to Health |
|---|---|---|
| Dental X-ray | 0.1 | Very low |
| Background radiation per year | 3 | Safe |
| Computerised Tomography (CT) scan | 15 | Considered an acceptable risk |
| Exposure to medium radioactive waste | 100 | Lowest level that causes a measured increased risk of cancer |
| Inside the tsunami and earthquake-damaged nuclear plant in Fukushima, Japan, in 2011 | 400 | Serious risk of developing cancer |

## Quick Test

1. What particles are found in the nucleus?
2. Name the three types of ionising radiation.
3. What is the type of radiation that passes through paper but is stopped by 3mm of aluminium?
4. Give two sources of background radiation.
5. What is meant by the term 'half-life'?
6. HT Describe an alpha particle.
7. HT A radioactive source has an activity of 288 counts per minute and a half-life of 6 hours. What will the activity be after 24 hours?
8. HT If a radioactive nucleus emits a beta particle, how does the nucleus change?

## HT Nuclear Fission

In a **chemical reaction** it's the electrons that cause the change. The elements involved stay the same but join up in different ways.

**Nuclear fission** takes place in the nucleus of the atom and different elements are formed:

- A **neutron** is absorbed by a large and unstable uranium nucleus. This splits the nucleus into two roughly equal-sized, smaller nuclei. This releases energy and more neutrons.
- A fission reaction releases far more energy than even the most **exothermic** chemical reactions. Once fission has taken place, the neutrons can be absorbed by other nuclei and further fission reactions can take place. This is a **chain reaction**.
- A chain reaction occurs when there's enough **fissile material** to prevent too many neutrons escaping without being absorbed. This is called **critical mass** and ensures every reaction triggers at least one further reaction.

Only uranium and plutonium can undergo nuclear fission in this way.

Neutron ○

Uranium nucleus

Nucleus now unstable     Fission occurs (splitting)

Krypton nucleus     **Energy**     Barium nucleus

Further neutrons

## The Nuclear Reactor

**Nuclear power stations** use fission reactions to generate the heat needed to produce **steam**. The **nuclear reactor** controls the chain reaction so that the energy is steadily released.

Fission occurs in the **fuel rods** and causes them to become very hot.

The **coolant** is a fluid pumped through the reactor. The coolant heats up and is then used in the **heat exchanger** to turn water into steam.

**Control rods**, made of **boron**, absorb neutrons, preventing the chain reaction getting out of control. Moving the control rods in and out of the **reactor core** changes the amount of fission that takes place.

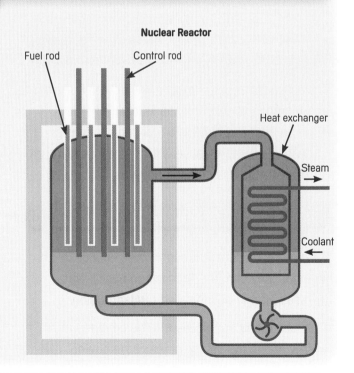

**Nuclear Reactor**

Fuel rod     Control rod

Heat exchanger

Steam

Coolant

# P6 Radioactive Materials

## Alpha Particle Scattering Experiment

At the beginning of the 20th century, discoveries about the nature of the atom and nuclear processes began to answer the mystery of the source of the Sun's energy.

In 1911, there was a ground-breaking experiment – the Rutherford–Geiger–Marsden alpha particle scattering experiment. In this experiment a thin **gold foil** was bombarded with alpha particles. The effect on the **alpha particles** was recorded and these observations provided the evidence for our current understanding of atoms.

Three observations were recorded:
- Most alpha particles were seen to **pass straight through** the gold foil.
- Some particles were **deflected** slightly.
- A few particles **bounced back** towards the source.

Particles passing through the foil indicated that gold atoms are composed of large amounts of space. The deflection and bouncing back of particles indicated that these alpha particles passed close to something positively charged within the atom and were repelled by it.

**The Gold Foil Scattering Experiment**

Alpha particle

Most particles passed straight through

Some particles were deflected back

Gold atom

Some particles were deflected slightly

## Conclusions of the Experiment

The observations of this experiment brought Rutherford and Marsden to conclude the following points:
- Gold atoms, and therefore all atoms, consist largely of empty space with a small, dense core. They called this core the **nucleus**.
- The nucleus is positively charged.
- The **electrons** are arranged around the nucleus with a great deal of space between them.

## The Nucleus of an Atom

If hydrogen nuclei are brought close enough together, they can fuse into helium nuclei. This releases energy and is called **nuclear fusion**.

This fusion process releases large amounts of energy and is the source of the Sun's power.

HT We now know that the nucleus contains **positive protons** and **neutral neutrons** held together by the short-ranged **strong nuclear force**. This force balances the repulsive electrostatic force between the protons.

**Key Words** | **Nucleus • Electron**

## Nuclear Energy

The amount of energy released during nuclear fission is much greater than that released in a chemical reaction involving a similar mass of material.

(HT) Einstein's equation states that for a mass of matter, *m*, the amount of energy, *E*, produced during nuclear fusion or fission is given by:

$$E = mc^2 \quad \text{where } c \text{ is the speed of light in a vacuum}$$

### Example 1

How much energy was generated from a uranium fuel rod if 2kg of the fuel was 'used up' during the fission process?

Using $E = mc^2$

$$E = 2 \times (3 \times 10^8)^2$$
$$= 2 \times 9 \times 10^{16}$$
$$= \textbf{18} \times \textbf{10}^{16} \textbf{ joules}$$

### Example 2

How much energy is released in the Sun, from the fusion of hydrogen atoms to form one helium atom, if the loss of mass is $4.75 \times 10^{-29}$kg?

Using $E = mc^2$

$$E = 4.75 \times 10^{-29} \times (3 \times 10^8)^2$$
$$= 4.75 \times 10^{-29} \times 9 \times 10^{16}$$
$$= \textbf{4.28} \times \textbf{10}^{-12} \textbf{ joules}$$

## (HT) Nuclear Equations

A radium nucleus decays by emitting an alpha particle. A new element is formed, which is called radon:

$$^{226}_{88}\text{Ra} \longrightarrow {}^{222}_{86}\text{Rn} + {}^{4}_{2}\text{He}$$

A **radioactive** carbon nucleus decays by emitting a beta particle:

$$^{14}_{6}\text{C} \longrightarrow {}^{14}_{7}\text{N} + {}^{0}_{-1}\text{e}$$

Note that gamma rays are just a form of energy. They don't change either the **atomic number**, or the mass number, when released from a radioactive nucleus.

## Quick Test

1. How is intermediate-level waste stored?
2. What particles were used to bombard the gold foil in the Rutherford–Geiger–Marsden experiment?
3. What conclusion was made about the nucleus from the Rutherford–Geiger–Marsden experiment?
4. (HT) What element is used in control rods in a nuclear reactor?
5. (HT) What elements can be used in a nuclear power station fuel rod?

# P6 Exam Practice Questions

1. Four students are talking about ionising radiation.

**Melanie**
I live in an area with high radon gas, which is a concern.

**Dol**
Ionising radiation comes from the nucleus of unstable atoms.

**Nathan**
Gamma can be used to treat cancer.

**Liam**
Alpha is easily absorbed by cells.

**(a)** Which **two** students are considering the risks of ionising radiation? Put ticks (✓) in the boxes next to the two correct answers. **[1]**

Melanie ⬭  Dol ⬭  Nathan ⬭  Liam ⬭

**(b)** Which **two** students are talking about sources of background radiation? Put ticks (✓) in the boxes next to the two correct answers. **[1]**

Melanie ⬭  Dol ⬭  Nathan ⬭  Liam ⬭

2. Draw a straight line from each term to the statement that best explains the term. **[2]**

| Term | Statement |
| --- | --- |
| Half-life | Measurement of a radiation dose's potential to harm a patient |
| Sievert | Rate of emission of radiation from the nucleus |
| Activity | Measurement of the time it takes for activity to drop by a half |

3. Rutherford, Geiger and Marsden carried out an alpha particle scattering experiment with gold. Explain what conclusions they came to about atoms as a result of the experiment. **[6]**

🖉 *The quality of written communication will be assessed in your answer to this question.*

..............................................................................................................................................................

..............................................................................................................................................................

..............................................................................................................................................................

..............................................................................................................................................................

..............................................................................................................................................................

..............................................................................................................................................................

..............................................................................................................................................................

**4** Nuclear power stations are still seen as a main source of energy in the UK but a nuclear reactor will need fuel rods to be replaced when they still contain 90% uranium.

**(a)** Give one advantage and one disadvantage of nuclear power stations. **[2]**

..................................................................................................................................................

..................................................................................................................................................

**(b)** Why are spent fuel rods sent away to be reprocessed rather than treated as nuclear waste? **[1]**

..................................................................................................................................................

..................................................................................................................................................

**HT** **5** **(a)** What is a chain reaction? **[6]**

🖉 *The quality of written communication will be assessed in your answer to this question.*

..................................................................................................................................................

..................................................................................................................................................

..................................................................................................................................................

..................................................................................................................................................

..................................................................................................................................................

..................................................................................................................................................

..................................................................................................................................................

..................................................................................................................................................

**(b)** There are several isotopes of uranium. What is an isotope? **[1]**

..................................................................................................................................................

..................................................................................................................................................

**(c)** An isotope of uranium has an atomic number of 92 and a mass number 238. It decays by emitting an alpha particle. What will be the atomic number and mass number of the element formed as a result of the decay? **[1]**

..................................................................................................................................................

**(d)** During the nuclear decay of uranium, the mass decreases by 0.05g. How much energy was released? **[2]**

..................................................................................................................................................

..................................................................................................................................................

**(e)** In an atomic nucleus, there is a strong repulsive force between the protons and the neutrons. Why doesn't the nucleus disintegrate? **[1]**

..................................................................................................................................................

## Looking into Space

The Earth fully rotates **west–east** on its axis once in just under 24 hours.

We can't feel the Earth spinning, but it is this rotation that makes the stars **appear** to move **east–west** across the sky once in just under 24 hours.

The Sun, planets and Moon also appear to travel east–west across the sky. Their motion, and the time they take to cross the sky, is affected by their relevant orbits. The Sun appears to travel across the sky once every 24 hours.

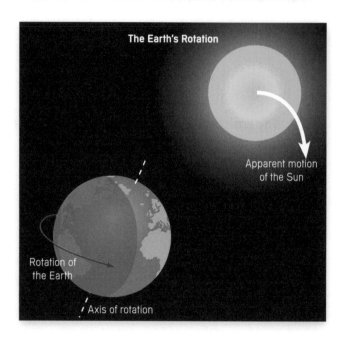

The Earth's Rotation

Apparent motion of the Sun

Rotation of the Earth

Axis of rotation

## (HT) The Earth and the Sun

A **sidereal day** is the time it takes for the Earth to rotate 360° on its axis. A **solar day** is the time from noon on one day to noon on the next day, i.e. 24 hours.

Whilst the Earth rotates once on its axis, it also orbits the Sun. It is this **orbiting** movement that makes a sidereal day **shorter** than a solar day.

Look at the diagram:
1. The Sun is directly over a point on the Earth.
2. The Earth has rotated 360°, but as it's also orbiting the Sun, the Sun is no longer directly overhead.
3. The Earth has had time to rotate a bit more so the Sun is now directly overhead, making the solar day longer than the sidereal day.

A sidereal day is 4 minutes shorter than a solar day.

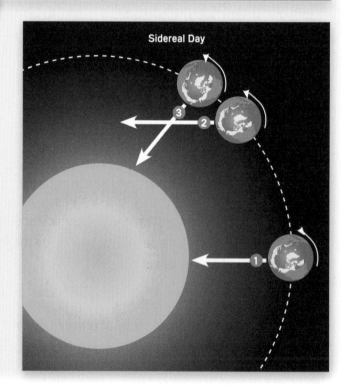

Sidereal Day

## The Position of the Stars

The Earth orbits around the Sun. An observer looking at the night sky from the Earth can see different stars at different times of the year.

Which stars are seen will depend on the Earth's position in relation to the Sun's position.

## Plotting Astronomical Objects

The position of an astronomical object can be measured in terms of **angles** as seen from the Earth. The angles of **declination** and **right ascension** describe the positions of the stars relative to a fixed point on the equator.

(HT) Declination is measured south and north of the celestial equator but right ascension is measured around the celestial equator.

A star with a…
- **positive declination** will be visible from the **northern hemisphere**
- **negative declination** will be visible from the **southern hemisphere**.

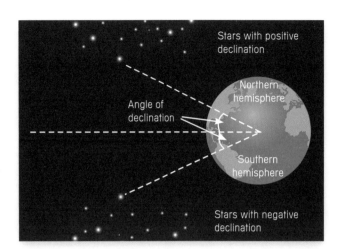

## The Planets

Mercury, Venus, Mars, Saturn and Jupiter can be seen from Earth with the naked eye.

From Earth, the planets look similar to stars. But the planets change their positions in complicated patterns when compared to the background of fixed stars. The planets sometimes appear to move with **retrograde motion** relative to the fixed stars.

(HT) We can see how the planets change their positions by using observations of **Venus** as an example. Venus is closer to the Sun than the Earth, so it orbits the Sun more quickly than the Earth does. If Venus is observed over a long enough period of time (e.g. one month), it can be seen to **move compared** to the **background stars**.

1. When Venus is on the same side of the Sun as the Earth, it looks like it's travelling in one direction against the background stars.
2. When Venus is on the other side of the Sun to the Earth, it looks like it's travelling in the opposite direction.

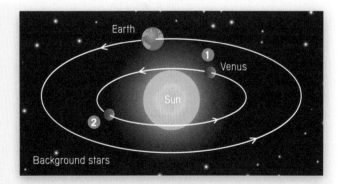

The planets generally appear to move in one direction across the sky relative to the background of stars. The Earth's smaller orbit causes it to overtake each of the outer planets at different times of the year, leading to the planets appearing to slow down against the star background and go into reverse. This is called **retrograde motion**.

## The Earth and the Moon

Whilst the Earth is rotating on its axis, the Moon is orbiting the Earth in the same direction.

Due to this orbiting movement, the Moon **appears** to travel **east–west** across the sky in a little over 24 hours.

For example, imagine you saw the Moon directly above you at a certain time one night. If you looked up again after one complete rotation of the Earth, the Moon wouldn't yet be directly above you. This is because the Earth's rotation wouldn't have yet caught up with the Moon's new orbital position.

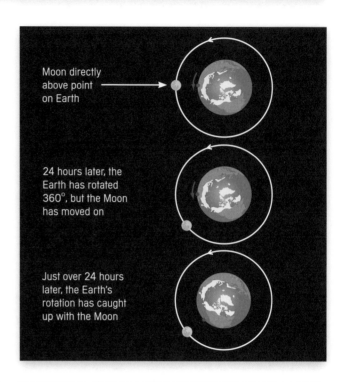

Moon directly above point on Earth

24 hours later, the Earth has rotated 360°, but the Moon has moved on

Just over 24 hours later, the Earth's rotation has caught up with the Moon

## The Lunar Cycle

The **lunar cycle** describes the Moon's appearance during its 28-day orbit of the Earth. The Moon's shape during this orbit is due to the part of the Moon that's **visible** from Earth.

We're able to see the Moon because the Sun's light is reflected from it. The side of the Moon **facing away** from the Sun appears **dark**, and the side **facing towards** the Sun appears **light**.

During the Moon's orbit around the Earth we can see different faces of the Moon:
- Dark face (new Moon)
- Light face (full Moon)
- All the points in between the new Moon and the full Moon.

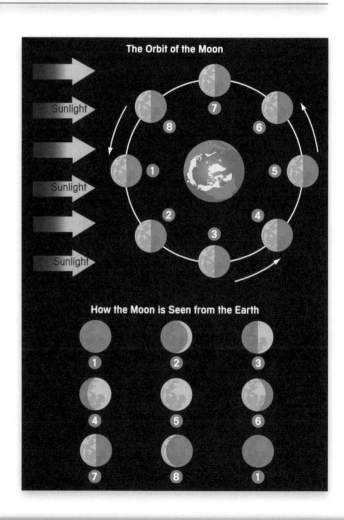

**The Orbit of the Moon**

Sunlight

Sunlight

Sunlight

**How the Moon is Seen from the Earth**

## Solar and Lunar Eclipses

A **solar eclipse** occurs when the **Moon passes** between the **Earth** and the **Sun**. This can happen during a new Moon and it results in the Moon casting **a shadow** on the Earth.

A **total solar eclipse** occurs when the Moon is directly in front of the Sun and completely obscures the Earth's view of the Sun. Observing solar eclipses directly can damage the eye.

A **lunar eclipse** occurs when the **Earth** is between the **Sun** and the **Moon**. This results in the Earth casting **a shadow** on the Moon.

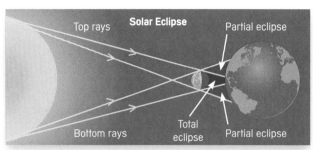

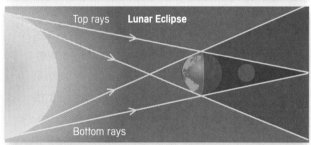

## HT Frequency of Eclipses

Eclipses don't occur every month because the Moon doesn't orbit the Earth in the same plane as the Earth orbits the Sun. (The Moon's orbit is inclined 5° to that of the Earth.)

So, an eclipse can only occur when the Moon passes through the **ecliptic** (the apparent path the

Sun traces out along the sky). This is more likely to occur when the Moon is to the **side of the Earth**, rather than **between** the Earth and the Sun.

There are between two and five solar eclipses every year, but a total eclipse will only occur roughly every 18 months.

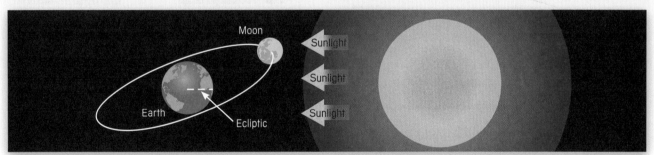

## Quick Test

1. What makes the stars appear to move from east to west?
2. What two angles describe the positions of a star?
3. What is a lunar eclipse?
4. HT What is a sidereal day?
5. HT Why don't eclipses occur every month?

# P7 Further Physics – Studying the Universe

## Behaviour of Waves

Light, water and sound waves can be...
- **refracted**
- **diffracted**.

**Refraction** – when waves cross a boundary between one medium and another, the **frequency** remains the same but there is a change in **wavelength**. This leads to a change in wave speed, which causes the wave to change direction.

**Diffraction** – when waves move through a narrow gap or past an obstacle, they spread out from the edges. This is called diffraction. Diffraction is most obvious when...
- the size of the gap is similar to, or smaller than, the wavelength of the wave
- the waves that pass obstacles have long wavelengths.

Light waves need a very small gap to be diffracted.

The fact that light and sound can be diffracted provides evidence of their wave nature.

**HT** Radiation is diffracted by the aperture of a telescope. To produce sharp images, the aperture must be very much larger than the wavelength of the radiation detected by the telescope.

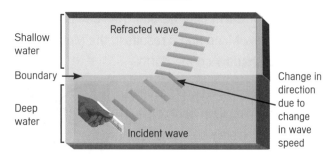

**Refraction**

Shallow water

Refracted wave

Boundary →

Deep water

Incident wave

Change in direction due to change in wave speed

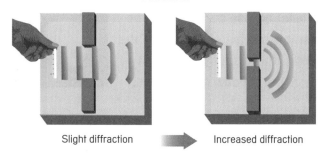

**Diffraction**

Slight diffraction → Increased diffraction

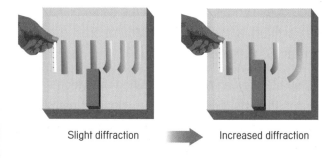

**Diffraction**

Slight diffraction → Increased diffraction

## Refraction of White Light

The colours that make up white light are refracted by different amounts as they pass through a prism:
- Red light is refracted the least.
- Violet light is refracted the most.

This refraction occurs because the colours that make up white light have different frequencies and different wavelengths.

A spectrum can also be produced when white light passes through a diffraction grating.

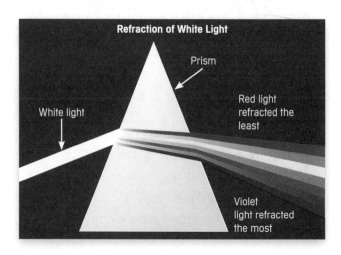

**Refraction of White Light**

Prism

White light

Red light refracted the least

Violet light refracted the most

Refraction • Diffraction • Frequency • Wavelength

## Convex Lenses

A **convex** (or converging) lens bends rays of light **inwards** as they pass through the lens. If the rays of light entering the lens are parallel, the rays will be brought to a **focus** at the **focal point**. This is due to refraction.

The greater the curvature of a lens, the more powerful it will be. So, if two lenses are made of the **same material**, a highly curved lens will be more powerful than a flatter lens.

You can calculate the power of a lens using this formula:

$$\text{Power (dioptres)} = \frac{1}{\text{Focal length (metres)}}$$

The **focal length** is the distance between the focal point and the lens.

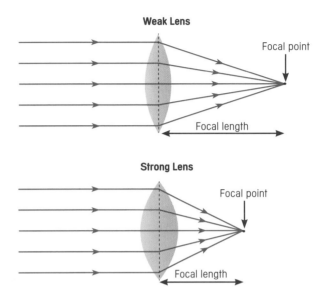

**Weak Lens**
Focal point
Focal length

**Strong Lens**
Focal point
Focal length

## Ray Diagrams

Ray diagrams show how the image of an object would be formed.

You may be required to interpret ray diagrams for convex/converging lenses gathering light from distant point sources (stars).

(HT) You need to be able to draw ray diagrams for the formation of **real images** from a…
- **distant point** source (stars)
- **distant extended** source (planets, galaxies and moons in our solar system). The image produced will be **inverted** and **smaller**.

1. Draw a ray line (Ray 1) that runs from the top of the object parallel to the principal axis. At the middle of the lens, bend this ray inwards so it passes through the focal point (F).
2. Draw a second ray (Ray 2) that runs from the top of the object straight through the centre of the lens as it crosses the principal axis.
3. Draw a third ray (Ray 3) that runs from the top of the object through the focal point on the same side as the object. When the ray hits the centre of the lens, bend it to travel parallel to the principal axis.
4. If the object crosses the principal axis, draw another ray (Ray 4) that runs from the bottom of

the object parallel to the principal axis. At the middle of the lens, bend this ray inwards so it passes through the focal point.

5. The image is formed where the rays meet.

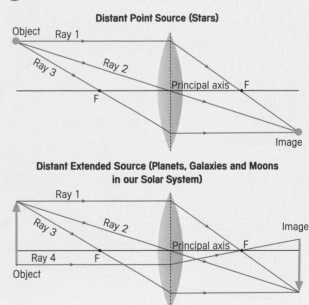

**Distant Point Source (Stars)**
Object
Ray 1
Ray 3
Ray 2
Principal axis F
F
Image

**Distant Extended Source (Planets, Galaxies and Moons in our Solar System)**
Ray 1
Ray 3
Ray 2
Image
Principal axis F
Ray 4
F
Object

# P7 Further Physics – Studying the Universe

## Telescopes

Objects in space are so far away that rays of light from them seem to be parallel. So, we draw the rays of light entering telescopes as parallel rays.

A **simple refracting telescope** is made from two converging lenses of different powers. The **eyepiece lens** is a higher power lens than the **objective lens**.

The objective lens captures parallel light from a distant object and brings it to a point on the focal point of the lens. This point is also the focal point for the eyepiece so the image acts as an object for the eyepiece, which magnifies it.

The distance between the lenses will be equal to the sum of the focal lengths of the objective and eyepiece lenses.

An **astronomical (reflecting) telescope** normally uses a **concave mirror** for the objective lens instead of a **convex lens**. This allows them to be larger, which means they can collect more light.

**Concave** mirrors reflect rays of parallel light and bring them to a focus.

The larger the telescope, the more light it captures and the more detail that will be visible in the image.

There will not be much light from distant or faint sources, so a large telescope will be needed to have any chance of seeing any useful details.

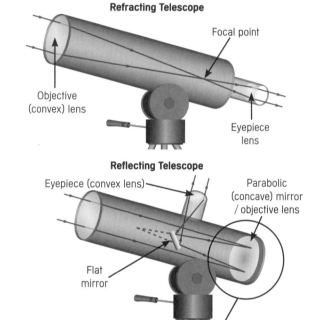

## HT Angular Magnification

The image of a **distant magnified object** will appear closer than the object. So, the angle made by ray lines entering the eye is greater.

This increase in angle is called the angular magnification and makes the image appear bigger / closer.

**Angular Magnification (as seen through a telescope)**

Apparent size of object

Large angle

You can calculate the angular magnification of a telescope using this formula:

$$\text{Magnification} = \frac{\text{Focal length of objective lens}}{\text{Focal length of eyepiece lens}}$$

### Example

The objective lens of a telescope has a focal length of 10m, and the eyepiece has a focal length of 2m. Calculate the magnification.

$$\text{Magnification} = \frac{\text{Focal length of objective lens}}{\text{Focal length of eyepiece lens}}$$

$$= \frac{10m}{2m}$$

$$= \times 5$$

## Parallax

**Parallax** can be thought of as the **apparent motion** of an object against a background.

However, it's actually the **motion of the observer** that causes the parallax motion of an object.

A simple way to observe parallax is if you hold your hand out in front of you with your thumb sticking up and alternately close one eye then the other. Although your thumb appears to move, in reality you're just looking at it from a **different angle**.

## Measuring Distance Using Parallax

Parallax can make a star **appear to move** in relation to the other stars in the course of a year.

In the diagram below, if an observer at **position ❶** looks at a near star compared to the distant background, it **appears** to be at **position B**. But if the observer then looks at the same star six months later (**position ❷**), the star **appears** to be at **position A**.

It looks as though the star has moved, but it's actually the **movement** of the **Earth's orbit** around the Sun that causes the observer to see this 'change in position'.

The **parallax angle (θ)** of a star is **half the angle** moved against a **background of distant** stars in **six months**.

An object that's further away from the Earth will have a smaller parallax angle than a closer object.

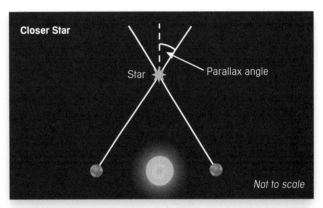

Closer Star — Star — Parallax angle — *Not to scale*

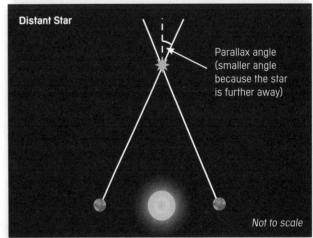

Distant Star — Parallax angle (smaller angle because the star is further away) — *Not to scale*

**Parallax** — A — T — B — Near star parallax motion — Near star — Parallax angle — θ — ❶ — ❷ — Earth's motion around the Sun — *Not to scale*

## Quick Test

1. What changes when waves cross the boundary between one medium and another and are refracted?
2. What is the power of a lens with a focal length of 0.2m?
3. Why is a mirror usually used in an astronomical telescope?
4. **HT** A refracting telescope has a magnification of ×3. If the focal length of the objective lens is 0.6m, what is the focal length of the eyepiece?

# P7 Further Physics – Studying the Universe

## Using Parallax

Astronomers use parallax to measure **interstellar** distances using the unit **parsec** (**pc**). The typical interstellar distance between stars is a few parsecs.

A parsec is the **distance to a star** with a **parallax angle** of one **second of an arc**. It's of a similar size to a **light-year**.

Astronomers can use the **megaparsec** (**Mpc**) to measure **intergalactic** distances even though these objects are so far away that the parallax angle is too small to measure.

For example, the nearest major galaxy, Andromeda, is 770 000 parsecs (0.77Mpc) away.

You can calculate the distance in parsecs using this formula.

$$\text{Distance (parsecs)} = \frac{1}{\text{Parallax angle (arcseconds)}}$$

### Example
The second-nearest star to Earth is Proxima Centauri. Astronomers found that it has a parallax angle of 0.77 arcseconds. Calculate its distance from the Earth.

$$\text{Distance} = \frac{1}{\text{Parallax angle}}$$

$$= \frac{1}{0.77 \text{ arcseconds}}$$

$$= \textbf{1.3 parsecs}$$

## Measuring Distance Using Brightness

Astronomers can also measure the distance to stars by observing how **bright** the stars are.

In theory, this method sounds very simple, i.e. a **close** star will **appear brighter** than a **more distant** star. But stars don't necessarily have the same **luminosity** (the amount of energy a star gives out).

A star's luminosity depends on its...
*   size
*   temperature.

A large or hot star will emit more light than a small or cool star. It may **appear brighter** even though it's **further away**.

So, the **observed intensity** of a star depends on its...
*   luminosity
*   distance from the Earth.

A star with a **low luminosity** may **appear dull** even if it's very close to the Earth. And a star with a very **high luminosity** may **appear bright** even if it's very far from the Earth.

For example, the star Antares is 500 light-years from the Earth. Although there are 100 000 stars closer to Earth than Antares, this star has a luminosity 10 000 times greater than that of the Sun and it's the 15th brightest star visible from Earth.

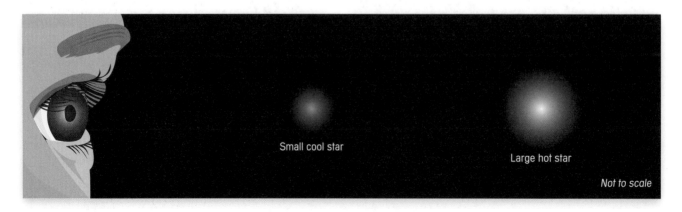

Small cool star

Large hot star

*Not to scale*

## Cepheid Variable Stars

A **Cepheid variable** star **doesn't** have a **constant** luminosity. It **pulses** and its luminosity depends on the period of the pulses. The period is equal to 1 ÷ frequency of the pulses.

This changing frequency can be used to work out the **distance** to Cepheid variable stars.

(HT) By measuring the frequency of the pulses, astronomers can estimate the star's luminosity. The **distance** to the star can then be worked out if we know…
- how bright the star **really is**
- how bright the star **appears**.

## The Curtis–Shapley Debate

In 1920, a great debate about the scale of the **Universe** took place between two prominent astronomers – Heber **Curtis** and Harlow **Shapley**.

Telescopes had revealed that the **Milky Way** contained lots of stars. This observation led to the realisation that the Sun was a star in the Milky Way **galaxy**.

Telescopes had also revealed many **fuzzy objects** in the night sky. These objects were originally called **nebulae** and they played a major role in the debate.

**Curtis** believed that the Universe consisted of many galaxies like our own, and the fuzzy objects were **distant galaxies**.

**Shapley** believed that the Universe contained only one big galaxy and the nebulae were nearby gas clouds **within the Milky Way**.

## Edwin Hubble

In the mid-1920s, Edwin Hubble observed **Cepheid variables** in one **nebula** and found that the nebula was **much further away** than any star in the Milky Way.

This observation provided the evidence that the observed nebula was a **separate galaxy**. This supported Curtis' idea that the Universe contains many different galaxies.

Observations of many Cepheid variables have shown that most nebulae are distant galaxies.

This has allowed astronomers to measure the distance to these galaxies, and so determine the **scale of the Universe**.

## The Hubble Constant

By observing Cepheid variable stars in distant galaxies, Edwin Hubble discovered that the Universe was **expanding**; in fact, the **further away** a star was, the **faster** it was **moving away**.

Cepheid variable stars in distant galaxies have been used to accurately calculate the **Hubble constant** because we know how far away they are.

So, we can use **red shift** to find out how fast they are moving away (their **speed of recession**).

Astronomers can now use the Hubble constant and red shift data to calculate the distance to other galaxies.

The speed of recession can be calculated using this formula:

$$\text{Speed of recession (km/s)} = \text{Hubble constant (s}^{-1})\text{ (km s}^{-1}\text{ Mpc}^{-1}) \times \text{Distance (km) (Mpc)}$$

### Example 1

A galaxy is a distance of $3 \times 10^{20}$km from Earth. If the Hubble constant is $2.33 \times 10^{-18}$ s$^{-1}$, calculate the speed of recession.

Speed of recession = Hubble constant × Distance

$$= (2.33 \times 10^{-18}\text{ s}^{-1}) \times (3 \times 10^{20}\text{km})$$

$$= \textbf{700km/s}$$

### Example 2

A galaxy is a distance of 10 megaparsecs from Earth. If the Hubble constant is 70km s$^{-1}$ Mpc$^{-1}$, calculate the speed of recession.

Speed of recession = 70km s$^{-1}$ Mpc$^{-1}$ × 10Mpc

$$= \textbf{700km/s}$$

*N.B. The speed of recession is the same in both examples. Example 1 uses distance in km and the Hubble constant in s$^{-1}$. Example 2 uses the astronomical unit of megaparsecs.*

### HT Example 3

Data from an observed galaxy gives the galaxy a speed of recession of 490km/s. Calculate the distance to the galaxy in both kilometres and megaparsecs.

Hubble constant = 70km s$^{-1}$ Mpc$^{-1}$ (or $2.33 \times 10^{-18}$ s$^{-1}$)

$$\text{Distance} = \frac{\text{Speed of recession}}{\text{Hubble constant}}$$

$$\text{Distance (km)} = \frac{490\text{km/s}}{2.33 \times 10^{-18}}$$

$$= \textbf{2.1} \times \textbf{10}^{20}\textbf{km}$$

$$\text{Distance (Mpc)} = \frac{490\text{km/s}}{70\text{km s}^{-1}\text{ Mpc}^{-1}}$$

$$= \textbf{7Mpc}$$

### Example 4

A nearby galaxy is 0.77Mpc from Earth and has a speed of recession of 54km/s. What is the Hubble constant?

$$\text{Hubble constant} = \frac{\text{Speed of recession}}{\text{Distance}}$$

$$= \frac{54\text{km/s}}{0.77\text{Mpc}}$$

$$= \textbf{70.1km s}^{-1}\textbf{ Mpc}^{-1}$$

# Further Physics – Studying the Universe P7

## Evidence for the Expansion of the Universe

Scientists believe that the Universe began with a huge explosion called the 'Big Bang' about 14 000 million years ago.

**HT** The spectra observed from elements in stars belonging to distant galaxies indicate that the light is red shifted. The more distant a galaxy, the more the light is red shifted. This is true in whichever direction an astronomer observes.

The motion of the galaxies suggests that space itself is expanding.

## Extrasolar Planets

**Extrasolar planets** are planets that orbit a star other than the Sun. Astronomers have found convincing evidence of hundreds of planets around nearby stars.

The first extrasolar planets to be discovered were large gas planets. As detection methods have become more sensitive, smaller planets similar to the size of the Earth have been found.

If even a small proportion of stars have planets, many scientists think that it's likely that life exists elsewhere in the Universe. However, no evidence of extraterrestrial life (at present or in the past) has so far been discovered by scientists.

### Quick Test

1. What two things does the observed intensity of a star depend on?
2. What does the brightness of a Cepheid variable depend on?
3. What did Shapley believe about the Universe?
4. What did Edwin Hubble discover about the Universe by observing Cepheid variable stars in distant galaxies?
5. **HT** A nearby galaxy is 0.88Mpc from Earth. If the Hubble constant is 70km s$^{-1}$ Mpc$^{-1}$, what is the speed of recession?
6. **HT** How can Cepheid variables be used to estimate the star's luminosity?

## Pressure and Volume

**Gas pressure** is caused by **particles** in a gas **moving about**. When a particle collides with an object, it exerts a force. This force is felt as pressure.

The amount of pressure depends on…
- the number of collisions per second
- the momentum of the particles.

As the volume of a gas is reduced, the particles have less room to move about. So, they collide with each other more often, **increasing the pressure.**

| | |
|---|---|
| **Pressure ✗ Volume = Constant** | This is only true if the temperature of the gas is constant. |

**Gas Inside a Piston**

Greater mass

5kg    10kg

Less volume so higher pressure

## Pressure and Temperature

If a gas is **heated up**, the particles move around **faster**. This increases their momentum and the force they exert when they collide with each other.

This could have two effects:

1 **Increase the volume** (by pushing the piston up).
2 **Increase the pressure** (if the volume is kept fixed).

*N.B. This effect also works in reverse, i.e. compressing a gas will cause it to increase in temperature.*

| | |
|---|---|
| $\dfrac{\text{Pressure}}{\text{Temperature}} = \text{Constant}$ | This is only true if the volume is constant. |
| $\dfrac{\text{Volume}}{\text{Temperature}} = \text{Constant}$ | This is only true if the pressure is constant. |

For a fixed mass of gas, both the pressure and the volume of the gas are proportional to the absolute temperature.

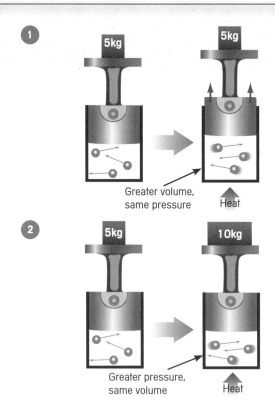

1

5kg    5kg

Greater volume, same pressure    Heat

2

5kg    10kg

Greater pressure, same volume    Heat

## Absolute Zero

As the **temperature** of a gas is **reduced**, the particles in the gas move **slower** and the **pressure falls**.

The particles eventually stop moving altogether. At this point the particles have no more energy to lose and the temperature can't get any lower. This occurs at -273°C, otherwise known as **absolute zero**.

**Absolute temperature** is a measure of temperature starting at absolute zero and is measured in **Kelvin (K)**.

To convert from…
- Kelvin into degrees Celsius, subtract 273
- degrees Celsius into Kelvin, add 273.

## The Structure of a Star

A star has three main parts:

- The **core** is the hottest part of the star where nuclear fusion takes place and energetic photons are released.
- The **convective zone** is where energy in the form of photons is transferred to the surface by convection currents.
- The **photosphere** is where the photons are radiated into space.

Like all hot objects, stars emit a continuous range of **electromagnetic** radiation. They emit radiation of a…

- **high luminosity**
- **high peak frequency** (i.e. frequency where most energy is emitted).

The luminosity and peak frequency increase with temperature.

An object that is red hot emits most of its energy in the red frequency range. The frequency of light given off from a star provides evidence of how hot it is.

**Structure of a Star**

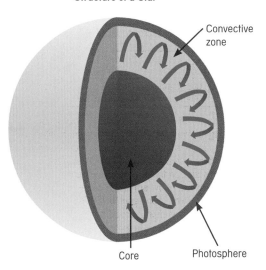

Convective zone

Core

Photosphere

## Using a Star's Spectrum

The **removal** of electrons from an atom is called **ionisation**. The **movement** of electrons within the atom causes it to emit radiation of specific frequencies called **line spectra**. Different elements have characteristic line spectra.

By comparing a star's spectrum to emission spectra from elements, we can see which chemical elements the star contains.

For example, the diagrams opposite compare the emission spectrum for hydrogen and the absorption spectrum that would be seen from the Sun.

The Sun's spectrum is complex, indicating that it contains more than one element. But, by comparing the spectra, we can see that the Sun contains hydrogen as well as some other elements (e.g. helium).

The absorption lines in the Sun's spectrum exactly match the emission lines from some elements produced in laboratory conditions.

**HT** Different electron energy levels in atoms give rise to line spectra. Electrons gain energy to move to a higher energy level and then release light of one wavelength only when they return to the lower energy level. As there are several possible moves in an atom, a series of lines with different wavelengths is emitted.

**Hydrogen Spectrum**   **The Sun's Spectrum**

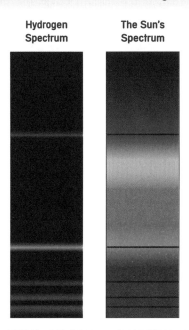

# P7 Further Physics – Studying the Universe

## The Beginning of a Star's Life

Stars begin as clouds of gas (mainly hydrogen). As **gravity** brings these gas clouds together, they become denser.

The force of gravity **pulls** the **gas inwards**, causing the pressure and temperature to increase. As more gas is drawn in, the force of **gravity increases**. This compresses the gas so that it becomes hotter and denser, and forms a **protostar**.

Eventually, the temperature and pressure become so high that the hydrogen nuclei fuse into helium nuclei. Energy is released in this **nuclear fusion** process. The star is now a stable **main sequence star**.

Nuclear processes discovered in the early 20th century provided a possible explanation of the Sun's energy source.

## Fusion in Stars

Most of the nuclear fusion occurs in the core of a star, where the temperature and density are highest. The more massive the star, the hotter its core and the heavier the nuclei it can create by fusion.

Energy is freed when light nuclei fuse. Heavier nuclei are made with masses up to that of the iron nucleus.

In the core of the Sun, as in all **main sequence** stars, hydrogen is fusing to form helium. When stars like our Sun leave the main sequence, they form **red giants**.

The core of a red giant is contracting and its temperature is rising. A further series of fusion reactions takes place:

- Helium fuses to form carbon.
- Further reactions produce heavier nuclei such as nitrogen and eventually oxygen.

$$3\,{}^{4}_{2}\text{He} \longrightarrow {}^{12}_{6}\text{C}$$

$$\,{}^{1}_{1}\text{H} + {}^{12}_{6}\text{C} \longrightarrow {}^{13}_{7}\text{N}$$

$$\,{}^{4}_{2}\text{He} + {}^{12}_{6}\text{C} \longrightarrow {}^{16}_{8}\text{O}$$

Energy is released at each stage. If the mass of the red giant is less than about three times the mass of the Sun, no more fusion reactions occur.

In a high mass star (several times the mass of the Sun), nuclear fusion can produce heavier nuclei up to and including iron. When the core is mostly iron, it explodes as a **supernova**, creating nuclei with masses greater than iron. A dense **neutron star** or **black hole** is produced.

## Hydrogen Burning in Main Sequence Stars

The equation boxes show how hydrogen nuclei fuse to produce helium nuclei with the release of energy. Notice that a positively charged particle is produced in the first stage. This is called a **positron** and has the mass of an electron. It has to be released to balance the charges in the reaction.

(HT) Einstein's equation $E = mc^2$ is used to calculate the energy released during nuclear fusion and fission. $E$ is the energy produced, $m$ is the mass lost and $c$ is the speed of light in a vacuum.

$$\,{}^{1}_{1}\text{H} + {}^{1}_{1}\text{H} \longrightarrow {}^{2}_{1}\text{H} + {}^{0}_{+1}\text{e} + \text{A neutrino which is a particle with no charge}$$

$$\,{}^{1}_{1}\text{H} + {}^{2}_{1}\text{H} \longrightarrow {}^{3}_{2}\text{He}$$

$$\,{}^{3}_{2}\text{He} + {}^{3}_{2}\text{He} \longrightarrow {}^{4}_{2}\text{He} + 2\,{}^{1}_{1}\text{H}$$

## The Life Cycle of a Star

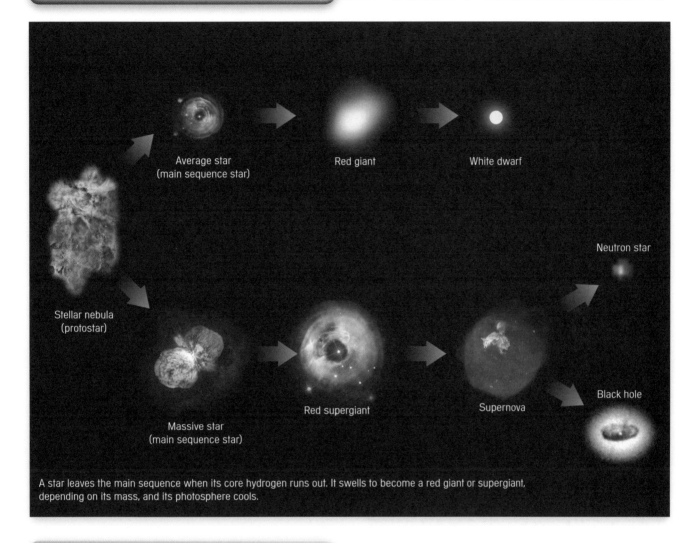

Average star
(main sequence star)

Red giant

White dwarf

Neutron star

Stellar nebula
(protostar)

Massive star
(main sequence star)

Red supergiant

Supernova

Black hole

A star leaves the main sequence when its core hydrogen runs out. It swells to become a red giant or supergiant, depending on its mass, and its photosphere cools.

## Hertzsprung–Russell Diagram

The **Hertzsprung–Russell diagram**…

- is a plot of temperature and luminosity
- identifies regions where supergiants, red giants, main sequence stars and white dwarfs are located.

A low mass star (similar to the Sun) becomes a **red giant**, which lacks the mass to compress the core further at the end of helium fusion.

It then shrinks to form a white dwarf, in which there's no nuclear fusion. The white dwarf gradually cools and fades.

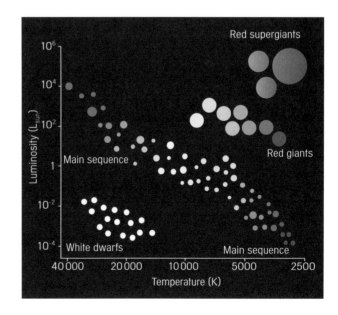

Red supergiants

Main sequence

Red giants

White dwarfs

Main sequence

# P7 Further Physics – Studying the Universe

## Ground-based Optical Telescopes

The major optical and infrared astronomical observatories on Earth are mostly situated in Chile, Hawaii, Australia and the Canary Islands. Two such observatories are the...

- **Royal Observatory** (the largest refracting optical telescope in the UK)
- **Mauna Kea Observatories**, Hawaii (the largest optical reflecting telescopes in the world).

**Astronomical factors** will often influence the choice of a site. For example, Hawaii has proven an ideal location because of its...

- **high altitude** (there's less atmosphere above it to absorb the light from distant objects)
- **isolated location** (there's less pollution to interfere with the received signal and there's sufficient distance from built-up areas that cause light pollution)
- **equatorial location** (which gives it the best view of solar eclipses)
- frequent cloudless skies.

There are other factors that should be considered when planning, building, operating or closing down an observatory. For example...

- cost
- environmental and social impact nearby
- working conditions for employees.

Mirrors for reflecting telescopes can be made much larger than lenses in a refracting telescope. The weight of the mirror is supported underneath rather than on the edges (as the weight of a lens is), so a mirror can have a greater weight without distorting.

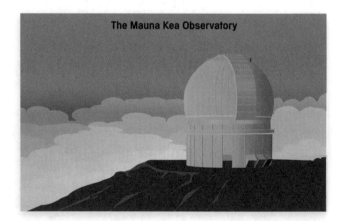
The Mauna Kea Observatory

## Space-based Telescopes

Space-based telescopes, e.g. the **Hubble telescope**, can obtain images of the Universe that can't be obtained in any other way.

Advantages of space telescopes include the following:

- They avoid the absorption and refraction effects of the Earth's atmosphere.
- They can use parts of the electromagnetic spectrum that the atmosphere absorbs.

Disadvantages of space telescopes include the following:

- They're very expensive to set up, maintain and repair.
- There are uncertainties associated with space programmes, e.g. launch delays.

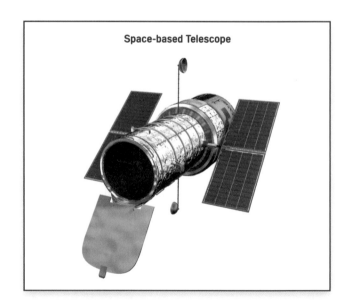
Space-based Telescope

## Advantages of Computer Control of Telescopes

There are several advantages of controlling a telescope from a computer:

- The telescope can be programmed to continually track certain objects. Data can be collected over a long period of time for analysis.
- The telescope can be situated in an isolated location which might normally be difficult to reach. Astronomers can control it from far away just as easily as if they were at the site of the observatory.
- The telescope can be programmed to precisely find any star, galaxy or other objects of astronomical interest by entering the coordinates of that object.
- The computer can directly record and process data collected.

## Funding Developments in Science

Most of the big new telescopes are developed through **international co-operation**. There are several advantages to this kind of joint venture:

- The **cost** of building the telescopes is **shared**.
- **Expertise** can be **shared**.
- Astronomers can book time on telescopes in different countries, allowing them to see the stars on other sides of the Earth.

For example, the Gemini Observatory in Chile (which opened in 2002) was the result of shared work between Australia and six other countries.

The Great Canary Telescope, in La Palma in the Canary Islands, allows astronomers to capture some of the most distant light in the Universe. This was mainly funded by the Spanish government but Mexico and the University of Florida in the USA also contributed.

These telescopes can be accessed...

- directly at the site
- through remote computer control (so astronomers don't have to travel to each telescope and can use it at convenient times)
- through the Internet (schools in the UK can access the Royal Observatory in this way).

## Quick Test

1. What two things does the pressure of a gas depend on?
2. What is the value of absolute zero?
3. How is energy transferred from the core of a star to the photosphere?
4. What information can be obtained by examining the Sun's spectrum?
5. What element is mainly present in the core of a star that becomes a supernova?
6. In the Hertzsprung–Russell diagram, what two types of star don't appear in the main sequence?
7. HT The speed of light is $3 \times 10^8$ m/s. How much mass must a star lose to radiate $1.8 \times 10^{17}$ joules of energy?

1. Four students are discussing the qualities of different types of telescope.

**Thu**
The telescope is expensive to repair.

**Evelyn**
The observatory in Hawaii was built at high altitude.

**Garvey**
The images have so much detail.

**Bonnie**
You need a large dish to receive radio waves.

(a) Which two students could have been discussing the Hubble telescope?
Put ticks (✓) in the boxes next to the **two** correct names. [1]

Thu ⬡  Evelyn ⬡  Garvey ⬡  Bonnie ⬡

(b) Which student was talking about a telescope that detects wavelengths longer than microwaves?
Put a tick (✓) in the box next to the correct name. [1]

Thu ⬡  Evelyn ⬡  Garvey ⬡  Bonnie ⬡

2. This question is about the behaviour of light. Use the words provided to complete the sentences. [4]

slow down    frequency    wavelength    speed up    a change
no change    waves    particles    refraction    reflection

When light waves pass from one medium to another, they can change direction. This is called

.......................................... . If light passes from air into glass, the light waves .......................................... and

the .......................................... becomes smaller. The .......................................... always remains the same.

There is usually .......................................... in the direction of travel.

3. Here is a table showing the total solar eclipses visible until 2020:

| Year | 2010 | 2012 | 2015 | 2016 | 2017 | 2019 |
|------|------|------|------|------|------|------|
| Date | July 11 | November 13 | March 20 | March 9 | August 21 | July 2 |
| Location | South America | Australia | Iceland / Northern Europe | Australia | North America | South America |

(a) How does a total solar eclipse occur? [1]

........................................................................................................

........................................................................................................

(b) What two conclusions can you draw from the table about eclipses? [2]

........................................................................................................

........................................................................................................

④ Which of the following statements are **true**? Put ticks (✓) in the boxes next to the **three** correct statements. **[3]**

When waves spread out after passing through a narrow gap, it's called diffraction. ☐

The larger the objective lens of a telescope, the more detail the image has. ☐

Cepheid variables pulse with a period related to their mass. ☐

Heber Curtis thought that spiral nebulae were part of the Milky Way. ☐

Scientists believe the Universe began with a 'Big Bang' 14 million years ago. ☐

If the volume of a gas at constant temperature is reduced, the pressure increases. ☐

⑤ A balloon containing gas has a volume of $80cm^3$ and is at a temperature of $20^{\circ}C$. If the balloon is placed in a water bath so that the gas is now heated to $60^{\circ}C$ at constant pressure, what will be the new volume of the balloon? **[2]**

..........................................................................................................................................................

..........................................................................................................................................................

(HT) ⑥ This question is about line spectra observed by astronomers.
Explain how line spectra are produced from stars, and how they can be used to identify the elements present in stars and give evidence to support the Big Bang theory. **[6]**

🖉 *The quality of written communication will be assessed in your answer to this question.*

..........................................................................................................................................................

..........................................................................................................................................................

..........................................................................................................................................................

..........................................................................................................................................................

..........................................................................................................................................................

..........................................................................................................................................................

..........................................................................................................................................................

⑦ **(a)** Why must the aperture of a telescope be much larger than the wavelength of the radiation detected in order to produce a sharp image? **[2]**

..........................................................................................................................................................

..........................................................................................................................................................

**(b)** What is the magnification of a telescope with an objective focal length of 40cm and an eyepiece of focal length 10cm? **[1]**

..........................................................................................................................................................

# Answers

## Module P1: The Earth in the Universe

### Quick Test Answers
#### Page 7
1. **Any three from:** He wasn't a geologist; Supporting evidence was limited; It could be explained more simply; The movement of continents wasn't detectable.
2. The decay of radioactive elements.
3. Fossils of plants and animals, and radioactivity of rocks.
4. P-waves
5. Subduction
6. Deep-floor spreading and the changing polarity of the Earth's magnetic field every million years.

#### Page 9
1. Longitudinal
2. 0.5m/s
3. Frequency
4. 10m

#### Page 13
1. Moons orbit planets; asteroids orbit the Sun.
2. Relative brightness and parallax
3. The wavelength increases (red shift).
4. The amount of mass in the Universe is hard to measure.
5. They're displaced towards the red end of the spectrum.
6. They're proportional to one another.

### Exam Practice Answers
1. (a) Toni; Tanya **[Both needed for 1 mark.]**
   (b) Ademola
2. (a) **Any two suitable answers, e.g.** Set up warning systems; Not allow multi-storey buildings to be built; Train emergency services to deal with rescue procedures, casualties and fires; Identify evacuation procedures; Ensure buildings have energy-absorbing foundations.
   (b) There were no major earthquakes for 68 years in San Francisco Bay **and** San Francisco lies near a fault line **should be ticked**.
3. The solar system is 5000 million years old; The Sun was born when nuclear fusion started in gas and dust clouds pulled together by gravity; **and** Pluto is no longer considered to be a planet **should be ticked**.
4. Amplitude – A measurement of how much energy a wave carries
   Frequency – The number of waves made per second by a source
   Wavelength – The distance between the corresponding points on two adjacent cycles
5. 36m/s
6. **This is a model answer which would score full marks:** P-waves are longitudinal, whereas S-waves are transverse waves. If the waves from an epicentre have to pass through the liquid region of the Earth's core to reach a detector, then only the P-waves will be detected as S-waves can't pass through molten regions. The refraction of waves due to their change of speed in different rock densities provides evidence for the structure of the Earth.
7. (a) Red shift is when the wavelength appears longer **[1]** due to a source of light moving away from the observer **[1]**.
   (b) Light from the galaxies was red shifted and the further away the galaxy, the greater the observed red shift **[1]**. This appeared to be the case in whichever direction astronomers observed the Universe **[1]**.
   (c) There is uncertainty over the amount of matter present **[1]** and not all the matter may be visible **[1]**.
8. Due to seafloor spreading **[1]** and the periodic reversal of the Earth's magnetic field **[1]**.

## Module P2: Radiation and Life

### Quick Test Answers
#### Page 19
1. Ultraviolet
2. Ultraviolet radiation; Gamma; X-rays
3. **Any two from:** The heating effect (sunburn); It can cause ageing of the skin; It can cause mutations; It can cause radiation poisoning.
4. A thin layer of gas in the Earth's upper atmosphere that absorbs some of the Sun's harmful ultraviolet radiation.
5. The radiation from the Earth has a lower principal frequency.
6. Some photons are scattered and reflected by other particles; Some photons are absorbed by particles; Photons spread out as they travel.

#### Page 23
1. An increase in the percentage of greenhouse gases, such as carbon dioxide, in the atmosphere.
2. They can travel huge distances without becoming significantly weaker.
3. Unwanted frequencies in a signal (random variations).
4. Analogue signals can have any value; digital signals only have two ('1' or '0').
5. Even with noise, it's clear which parts of the signal represent 1 and 0, so it can be regenerated without noise.
6. It is used with climate models to look for patterns in the possible causes of global warming.

### Exam Practice Answers
1. X-rays have a shorter wavelength than gamma rays **should be ticked**.
2. (a) Deqa **and** Evelyn **should be ticked. [Both needed for 1 mark.]**
   (b) Deqa **should be ticked**.
3. **Any suitable answer, e.g.** There is a positive correlation **[1]**. The data can be used to predict future values **[1]**.
4. Water molecules strongly absorb some microwave wavelengths **and** Microwaves in microwave ovens have a different wavelength to the ones used by mobile phones **should be ticked**.
5. (a) A digital signal
   (b) Digital signals only have two states, on (1) or off (0), so they can still be recognised despite any noise that's picked up **[1]**. This means any interference can be removed **[1]**.
   (c) **Any three from:** Hard drive; Memory stick; USB stick; DVD; CD; Floppy disk
6. (a) **This is a model answer which would score full marks:** The latest data for many different points on the Earth's surface, such as surface temperature, wind speed, cloud cover, atmospheric pressure, the percentage of carbon dioxide and methane at different altitudes and the temperature at different altitudes, can be fed into a computer model. By adding projected changes caused by human activities, the software model can be run on the computer and the outcomes studied to see the predicted effect of human activities on the climate.
   (b) Increased convection **[1]** and larger amounts of water vapour in the hotter atmosphere **[1]**.
7. With a digital signal affected by noise, it's still possible to read the two-state pattern of '1's and '0's, so the signal can be recovered **[1]**. With analogue signals having any value, noise completely changes some of the signal, making it almost impossible to recover **[1]**.

## Module P3: Sustainable Energy

### Quick Test Answers

**Page 29**
1. To reduce the energy losses.
2. **Any five from:** Coal; Gas; Oil; Nuclear; Wind; Water (hydroelectric, tidal, wave); Solar; Biofuel
3. Global warming; Climate change
4. By rotating a magnet near the coil.
5. Potential energy; Kinetic energy; Electrical energy

**Page 33**
1. 180J
2. 25%
3. 3kW

### Exam Practice Answers
1. (a) Joseph **should be ticked**.
   (b) Ozair **and** Joseph **should be ticked. [Both needed for 1 mark.]**
2. It's generated from another energy source such as fossil fuels or nuclear power.
3. (a) The generator rotates a magnet **[1]** in a coil to produce electricity **[1]**.
   (b) To cut energy losses in the wire as the current is reduced to a small value by stepping up the voltage. This reduces heat loss.
   (c) Steam from the heated water drives the turbine blades.
4. To show the generation and distribution of electricity **[1]**, including the efficiency of energy transfers **[1]**.

5. (a) (i) One that is windy **[1]** and exposed **[1]**. **[Accept 'without turbulence'.]**
       (ii) **Any suitable answer, e.g.** There's a consistent supply of wind; Households use the same quantity of electricity per year.
   (b) Kinetic to electrical.

6.

| Electrical Appliance | Energy In | Useful Energy Out | Efficiency |
|---|---|---|---|
| Iron | 2000 joules/s | Heat: 1600 joules/s | $\frac{1600}{2000} \times 100 = $ **80%** |
| Radio | 200 joules/s | Sound: 60 joules/s | $\frac{60}{200} \times 100 = $ **30%** |
| Computer | 400 joules/s | Light: 180 joules/s Sound: 80 joules/s | $\frac{260}{400} \times 100 = $ **65%** |

7. **This is a model answer which would score full marks:** Other countries could control both the cost and supply of gas to the UK, which wouldn't be in the country's interest. Also, a much larger mass of gas has to be burned in order to produce a similar amount of energy to a very small mass of nuclear fuel. Nuclear fuel comes from stable regions of the world and doesn't release greenhouse gases like burning gas does. Only a small mass of nuclear fuel is required to produce a high electrical output from a power station.

## Module P4: Explaining Motion

### Quick Test Answers

**Page 38**
1. It was zero – the speed was constant.
2. 20m North

**Page 45**
1. Action
2. 24kg m/s
3. Crumple zone; Seat belt; Air bag
4. $\frac{1}{2} \times 60 \times 4^2 = 480J$
5. 20m
6. 4m/s

### Exam Practice Answers
1. (a) A3; B2; C1 **[2 marks for all three correct, 1 mark for one correct]**
   (b) The speed
2. (a) 8m/s **should be ringed**.
   (b) 7.5m/s² **should be ringed**.
3. Speed–time graphs are used in lorry tachographs to make sure drivers rest for the appropriate time **and** Friction is a force that always opposes motion **should be ticked**.
4. **This is a model answer which would score full marks:** Without friction it would be impossible to walk. There is a frictional force that is experienced by the shoe and acts in the direction the person is walking in. The force experienced by the pavement is in the opposite direction and has the same magnitude. As the person wearing the shoe has a much smaller mass than the ground, the person moves forward relative to the ground.

5. (a) Momentum = 1500 × 45 = 67 500kg m/s
       **[1 mark for correct working but wrong answer]**
   (b) Acceleration = $\frac{55-45}{4}$ = 2.5m/s²
       **[1 mark for correct working but wrong answer]**
6. The change in momentum depends on the size of the force acting and the time it acts for **and** If the resultant force on a car is zero, its momentum is constant **should be ticked**.
7. PE lost = Weight × Height
   = 40 × 20 = 800J
   PE lost = KE gained
   $800 = \frac{1}{2}mv^2$
   $800 = \frac{1}{2} \times 4 \times v^2$
   $v = 20$m/s
   **[1 mark for correct working but wrong answer]**
8. (a) Change in momentum = 150 × 3 − (150 × -2) (Remember the velocity of rebound will be negative.)
       Change in momentum = 450 + 300 = 750kg m/s
       **[1 mark for correct working but wrong answer]**
   (b) Force × 0.5 = 750, so force = 1500N
       **[1 mark for correct working but wrong answer]**
   (c) To increase the impact time, which reduces the force on his body.

# Answers

## Module P5: Electric Circuits

**Quick Test Answers**

**Page 51**
1. Positive
2.
3. $4\Omega$
4. They're proportional.
5. 0.5A
6. There are more collisions between the flowing electrons and the vibrating ions, giving a higher resistance. This leads to more heat being produced by the resistor.

**Page 55**
1. The principle of electromagnetic induction.
2. 6W
3. A changing magnetic field.
4. 4000 turns
5. 0.25A

**Exam Practice Answers**
1. The two rods will attract each other.
2. —|⊢ **should be ringed.**
3. Lamp – 2A; Resistor – 30V; Coil – 6$\Omega$

## Module P6: Radioactive Materials

**Quick Test Answers**

**Page 62**
1. Protons and neutrons
2. Alpha; Beta; Gamma
3. Beta
4. **Any two from:** Radon gas; Medical; Food; Cosmic rays; Gamma rays; Nuclear industry
5. The time it takes for the radioactivity to halve.
6. An alpha particle is a helium nucleus and consists of two protons and two neutrons.
7. 18 counts per minute.
8. It has one more proton and one less neutron than the original nucleus.

**Page 65**
1. It is mixed with concrete and stored in big containers.
2. Alpha particles
3. Gold atoms (and therefore all atoms) consisted of mainly empty space with a small, dense core called the nucleus. The charge on the nucleus was positive.
4. Boron
5. Uranium or plutonium

**Exam Practice Answers**
1. (a) Melanie **and** Liam **should be ticked. [Both needed for 1 mark.]**
   (b) Melanie **and** Dol **should be ticked. [Both needed for 1 mark.]**
2. Half-life – Measurement of the time it takes for activity to drop by a half
   Sievert – Measurement of a radiation dose's potential to harm a person
   Activity – Rate of emission of radiation from the nucleus
   **[2 marks for all three correct; 1 mark for one correct.]**
3. **This is a model answer which would score full marks:**
   They concluded that an atom mostly consisted of empty space (a vacuum) because most alpha particles passed straight through the gold foil. The electrons were arranged around the nucleus of the atom with a great deal of space between them.

4. **Any two from:** Spin the magnet faster; Increase the number of turns on the coil; Use a stronger magnet.
5. (a) Jake **should be ticked.**
   (b) Jessie **and** Sonny **should be ticked. [Both needed for 1 mark.]**
6. (a) (i) Thermistor
       (ii) They're inversely proportional. **[Accept 'there is a negative correlation'.]**
   (b) **Any one from:** Read the ammeter incorrectly; Not put the thermistor in the ice; Not measured the temperature correctly.
   (c) Add a buzzer or bell in series with the battery and thermistor (and ammeter).
7. **This is a model answer which would score full marks:** An alternating potential difference across the primary coil produces an alternating magnetic field in the iron core. This alternating field passes backwards and forwards around the iron core and through the secondary coil, which has more turns than the primary coil. This induces an alternating potential difference across the secondary coil which will be higher than the input alternating voltage.
8. $\dfrac{3000}{\text{Secondary turns}} = \dfrac{150}{900}$

   So secondary turns = 18 000

Only some of the alpha particles were deflected or bounced back, suggesting that the nucleus was small, dense and positively charged. This made it difficult for alpha particles to knock out or interact with the nucleus.

4. (a) Advantage: **Any one from:** They don't produce carbon dioxide; They don't produce sulfur dioxide; They don't produce particulates.
   Disadvantage: **Any one from:** They produce radioactive waste; Risk of serious accident.
   (b) It makes sense to recycle the uranium and cut down on the radioactive waste that needs to be disposed of. **[Accept that it reduces the need to remove extra uranium from the ground.]**
5. (a) **This is a model answer which would score full marks:** A chain reaction is when a uranium (or plutonium) nucleus absorbs a neutron, becoming unstable. It then splits into two smaller nuclei, releasing energy and producing three more neutrons. There is enough fissile material to prevent too many neutrons escaping without being absorbed. This is the critical mass and ensures every reaction triggers at least one further reaction.
   (b) An isotope of an element has the same number of protons (atomic number) as that element but a different number of neutrons.
   (c) The atomic number will be 90 and the mass number will be 234. **[Both must be correct for 1 mark.]**
   (d) $E = mc^2 = \dfrac{0.05}{1000} \times (3 \times 10^8)^2 = 4.5 \times 10^{12}$J
   **[1 mark for correct working but wrong answer].**
   (e) The strong nuclear force opposes and balances the force of repulsion.

# Answers

## Module P7: Further Physics – Studying the Universe

### Quick Test Answers

**Page 71**

1. The rotation of the Earth from west to east.
2. The angles of declination and right ascension.
3. When the Earth passes directly between the Sun and the Moon, casting a shadow onto the Moon.
4. The time taken for the Earth to rotate 360° on its axis.
5. The Moon doesn't orbit the Earth in the same plane as the Earth orbits the Sun.

**Page 75**

1. The speed of the wave and the wavelength.
2. Power = $\frac{1}{0.2}$ = 5 dioptres
3. It can be made larger than a lens and therefore gathers more light. This gives greater detail in the image.
4. 0.2m

**Page 79**

1. Luminosity and distance from the Earth.
2. The frequency/period of the pulses.
3. Shapley believed the Universe contained only one big galaxy.
4. Hubble discovered that the Universe was expanding.
5. Distance × Hubble constant = Speed of recession
   0.88Mpc × 70km s$^{-1}$ Mpc$^{-1}$ = Speed of recession
   61.6km/s = Speed of recession
6. By measuring the frequency of the pulses.

**Page 85**

1. The number of collisions per second between the particles and the walls of the container; The momentum of the particles.
2. -273°C
3. By convection and photons of radiation.
4. The elements present in the Sun.
5. Iron
6. White dwarfs and red giants [accept 'red supergiants'].
7. 2kg

### Exam Practice Answers

1. (a) Thu **and** Garvey **should be ticked. [Both needed for 1 mark.]**
   (b) Bonnie **should be ticked**.
2. refraction; slow down; wavelength; frequency; a change
   **[4 marks for all five correct; 3 marks for four correct; 2 marks for three correct; 1 mark for two correct]**
3. (a) When the Moon passes between the Sun and Earth, completely obscuring the Earth's view of the Sun.
   (b) Total solar eclipses don't occur frequently **[1]**. They can only be seen in a few locations when they occur **[1]**.
4. When waves spread out after passing through a narrow gap, it's called diffraction; The larger the objective lens of a telescope, the more detail the image has; **and** If the volume of a gas at constant temperature is reduced, the pressure increases **should be ticked**.
5. $\frac{V_1}{T_1} = \frac{V_2}{T_2}$
   So $\frac{80}{(20 + 273)} = \frac{V_2}{(60 + 273)}$
   $V_2 = 90.9m^3$
   **[1 mark for correct working but wrong answer]**
6. **This is a model answer which would score full marks:** Electrons in orbit around the nucleus in atoms gain energy and then release it as photons of light. For each type of atom, only certain values of energy can be absorbed and then re-emitted by the electrons as photons. This causes photons of different colours to be emitted, leading to spectra being seen. Each element emits its own set of spectral lines, so the element's emission spectra can then be matched with the absorption spectra seen in stars' spectra to identify which elements are present in the star. The spectral lines are red shifted, which indicates that the Universe is expanding.
7. (a) The aperture of a telescope causes diffraction **[1]**. By having a very large aperture compared to the wavelength of light, the diffraction effects are reduced to a level that can almost be ignored **[1]**, giving sharp images.
   (b) Magnification = $\frac{40}{10}$ = ×4

# Glossary of Key Words

**Absolute zero** – the lowest temperature possible.

**Acceleration** – the rate at which an object increases in speed.

**Air resistance** – the opposition to motion due to air friction.

**Alpha** – a radioactive particle made of two protons and two neutrons.

**Alternating current** – an electric current that changes direction of flow continuously.

**Amplitude** – the maximum disturbance caused by a wave.

**Analogue** – a signal that varies continuously in amplitude / frequency; can take any value.

**Atom** – the smallest part of an element that can enter into a chemical reaction.

**Beta** – a type of radioactive particle made of an electron.

**Big Bang** – a theory of how the Universe started.

**Bit** – the basic unit of information in digital signals; can be either '1' or '0'.

**Byte** – a sequence of eight bits used in digital signals to represent a number or character. To send the word 'eight' would require five bytes as there are five letters.

**Carbon cycle** – the constant recycling of carbon by the processes in life, death and decay.

**Cepheid variable** – a star that has a changing luminosity.

**Commutator** – part of an electric motor which is a segmented disk that rotates with the coil switching over the contacts with the two brushes. This keeps the current flowing in one direction through the magnetic field and ensures rotation of the coil.

**Contamination** – when clothes or a body absorb or become covered in radioactive material.

**Continental drift** – the movement of continents being carried on tectonic plates.

**Convection current** – warm fluid rises to be replaced with colder, denser fluid.

**Current** – the rate of flow of an electrical charge, measured in amperes (A).

**Decomposer** – an organism that breaks down other matter.

**Deforestation** – the destruction of forests by cutting down trees.

**Diffraction** – the spreading out of a wave as it passes an obstacle and expands into the region beyond the obstacle.

**Digital** – a signal that uses binary code to represent information; has two states: on (1) and off (0).

**Direct current** – an electric current that only flows in one direction.

**Distance–time graph** – a graph showing distance travelled against time taken; the gradient of the line represents speed.

**Eclipse** – the 'hiding' of one heavenly body behind another.

**Efficiency** – the useful energy output expressed as a percentage of total energy input.

**Electromagnetic spectrum** – a continuous arrangement that displays electromagnetic waves in order of increasing frequency.

**Electron** – a negatively charged subatomic particle that orbits the nucleus.

**Element** – a substance that consists of only one type of atom.

**Energy** – the ability of one physical system to do work on another physical system.

**Energy transfer** – the movement of energy from one place to another.

**Erosion** – the wearing away of the Earth's surface.

# Glossary of Key Words

**Extrasolar planet** – a planet that orbits a star other than the Sun.

**Field lines** – lines of force that, by definition, pass from the North pole of a magnet to the South pole.

**Focal length** – the distance between the focal point and the lens.

**Focal point** – the point at which all light rays parallel to the axis of the lens converge, or appear to converge.

**Force** – a push or pull acting upon an object.

**Frequency** – the number of times that something happens in a set period of time; the number of times a wave oscillates in one second; measured in hertz (Hz).

**Friction** – the resistive force between two surfaces as they move over each other.

**Galaxy** – a collection of stars and planets.

**Gamma** – a radioactive emission that is an electromagnetic wave.

**Generator** – a device in which a magnet spins inside a coil of wire to produce a voltage or an electric current.

**Geohazard** – any natural hazard associated with the Earth, e.g. an earthquake.

**Global warming** – the gradual increase in the average temperature on Earth.

**Gradient** – the steepness of the slope of a graph.

**Gravity** – a force of attraction between masses; the force that keeps objects orbiting larger objects.

**Greenhouse effect** – the process by which the Earth is kept warm by the atmosphere reflecting heat back down towards the Earth, preventing it from escaping into space.

**Half-life** – the time taken for half the radioactive atoms in a material to decay.

**Hertzsprung–Russell diagram** – a scatter graph of stars plotted to show the relationship between luminosity and temperature.

**Instantaneous speed** – the speed of an object at a particular point.

**Insulation** – material that is a poor conductor of heat.

**Ion** – a positively or negatively charged particle formed when an atom, or group of atoms, loses or gains electrons.

**Ionisation** – the removal of electrons.

**Irradiation** – when a person is exposed to radioactive emissions.

**Kinetic energy** – the energy possessed by an object because of its movement.

**Light-year** – the distance light travels in one year.

**Longitudinal wave** – an energy-carrying wave in which the movement of the particles is in line with the direction in which the energy is being transferred.

**Luminosity** – the brightness of a star, dependent on its size and temperature.

**Magnetic field** – a region where a force acts on a magnetic material placed there.

**Main sequence** – a part of the life cycle of stars that all stars pass through; it runs from the time stars are born as a hot protostar and continues up to the point that all the hydrogen has been used up by fusion.

**Memory stick** – a device for storing digital information in the form of bytes.

**Momentum** – a measure of state of motion of an object as a product of its mass and velocity.

**National Grid** – the high voltage electric power transmission network in the UK.

**Nebula** – an interstellar cloud of dust, hydrogen gas and plasma; another galaxy in the making.

**Neutron** – a particle found in the nucleus of an atom that has no electrical charge.

**Neutron star** – the extremely dense remainder of some of the largest stars.

**Noise** – unwanted frequencies in a signal that can distort it.

# Glossary of Key Words

**Nuclear fusion** – the joining together of two or more atomic nuclei to form a larger atomic nucleus.

**Nuclear waste** – the radioactive waste left over as a by-product of nuclear power generation.

**Nucleus** – the core of an atom, made up of protons and neutrons (except hydrogen, which contains a single proton).

**Observed intensity** – the brightness of a star, dependent on its luminosity and distance from Earth.

**Ozone layer** – the layer of gas in the upper atmosphere that absorbs ultraviolet radiation.

**Parallax** – the apparent movement of an object; movement is actually caused by motion of the observer.

**Peer review** – the process by which new scientific ideas and discoveries are validated by other scientists.

**Photon** – a 'packet' of energy carried by electromagnetic radiation.

**Photosynthesis** – the chemical process that takes place in green plants where water combines with carbon dioxide to produce glucose, using light energy.

**Potential difference** – the work done on or by per unit charge as it passes between two points in a circuit.

**Power** – the rate at which energy is converted from one form to another.

**Pressure** – force per unit area.

**Primary energy source** – an energy source found in nature that hasn't been converted in any way. Examples include fossil fuels and alternative sources of energy such as wind, water and solar.

**Proton** – a positively charged particle found in the nucleus of an atom.

**Radiation** – energy carried by gamma radiation or by a stream of particles such as neutrons, alpha particles or beta particles.

**Radioactive** – a material that decays by emission of alpha, beta or gamma radiation.

**Red giant** – a stage that a Sun-type star reaches when hydrogen fusion stops. The core collapses, heating up and causing the outer layers to expand.

**Red shift** – the shift of light towards the red part of the visible spectrum; shows that the Universe is expanding.

**Refraction** – the change in direction and speed of a wave as it passes from one medium to another.

**Renewable** – resources (e.g. energy sources) that will not run out or can be replaced.

**Resistance** – the measure of how hard it is to get a current through a component at a particular potential difference / voltage.

**Resultant force** – the total force acting on an object (the effect of all the forces combined).

**Retrograde motion** – the apparent backwards motion of planets from west to east due to the combined motion of the Earth and the planet.

**Risk** – the danger (normally to health) associated with a procedure, action or event.

**Seismograph** – an instrument to measure and show ground movement during an earthquake.

**Speed of light** – the speed at which light travels.

**Speed–time graph** – a graph showing speed against time taken; the gradient of the line represents acceleration.

**Static electricity** – a concentration of charge on an insulating material which is unable to move.

**Supernova** – an exploding star.

**Tectonic plate** – a huge section of the Earth's crust that moves in relation to another plate.

**Transformer** – an electrical device used to change the potential difference / voltage of alternating currents.

# Glossary of Key Words

**Transverse wave** – a wave in which the vibrations are at 90° to the direction of energy transfer.

**Turbine** – a generator that converts kinetic energy from the flow of water, air or steam into useful energy such as electricity.

**Universe** – a collection of galaxies.

**Velocity** – an object's speed and direction.

**Voltage** – a measurement of the potential difference between two points in a circuit.

**Wavelength** – the distance between corresponding points on two adjacent disturbances (waves).

**Work done** – work is done on a body or object when energy is transferred to it.

(HT) **Angular magnification** – a means of measuring the magnification based on the angle of rays of light from an object compared to the angle the image appears to make.

**Chain reaction** – a reaction, e.g. nuclear fission, that is self-sustaining.

**Ecliptic** – the apparent path the Sun traces out along the sky.

**Hubble's Law** – a law which states that the further away a galaxy is, the faster it is moving away from us.

**Isotope** – an atom of the same element that contains different numbers of neutrons.

**Nuclear fission** – the splitting of atomic nuclei, which is accompanied by a release in energy.

**Nuclear reactor** – the place where fission takes place in a nuclear power station.

**Real image** – an image produced by rays of light meeting at a point; an image that can be focused on a screen.

**Sidereal day** – the time it takes the Earth to rotate 360°.

**Solar day** – a full 24 hours.

**Subduction** – when an oceanic plate is forced under a continental plate.

**Uranium** – a radioactive element often used as nuclear fuel.

**Velocity–time graph** – a graph that shows how velocity (speed in a given direction) changes with time.

# Notes

**A**
Absolute zero 80
Acceleration 38, 39
Air resistance 44
Alpha particle scattering experiment 64
Amplitude 8
Angular magnification 74
Asteroid 10
Atom 58, 64, 81
Attraction 48

**B**
Big Bang 13, 79
Biofuel 27, 32
Bit 23
Byte 23

**C**
Carbon cycle 19
Chain reaction 63
Circuit 50
    parallel 52
    series 52
    symbols 49
Comet 10
Commutator 55
Contamination 26, 59, 61
Continental drift 5
Convection current 6
Convex lens 73, 74
Crater 4
Current 30, 48, 49–50, 51, 52, 53, 54, 55
    alternating 49, 54
    direct 49
Curtis–Shapley debate 77

**D**
Declination 69
Decomposer 19
Deforestation 19
Diffraction 72
Displacement–time graph 37
Distance–time graph 37, 38
Dwarf planet 10

**E**
Earthquake 5
Eclipse 71
Ecliptic 71
Einstein's equation 65, 82
Electromagnetic spectrum 16
Electromagnetic wave 21
Electron 48, 58, 59, 81
Element 58
Epicentre 6, 7
Erosion 4
Extrasolar planet 79
Eyepiece lens 74

**F**
Field line 55
Focal length 73, 74
Focal point 73, 74
Folding 4
Fossil fuel 32
Frequency 8, 9, 21, 72
Friction 40, 43

**G**
Generator 29, 53
Geohazard 5
Geothermal 27, 32
Global warming 20, 27
Gravitational potential energy 45
Gravity 10, 40, 44, 82
Greenhouse effect 18

**H**
Half-life 60
Hertzsprung–Russell diagram 83
Hubble constant 78
Hydroelectricity  28, 29, 32

**I**
Igneous rock 6
Instantaneous speed 36, 38
Insulation 33
Ion 17, 61
Ionisation 81
Irradiation 26, 59, 61
Isotope 58

**K**
Kinetic energy 43

**L**
Light dependent resistor 49, 51
Light-year 11, 76
Longitudinal wave 7, 8
Luminosity 76, 77, 83
Lunar cycle 70

**M**
Magnetic field 6, 53, 55
Memory stick 23
Metamorphic rock 6
Momentum 41–42

**N**
National Grid 26, 29
Nebula 77
Neutron 58, 59
Noise 22
Nuclear fission 63
Nuclear fusion 10, 64, 82
Nuclear reactor 63
Nuclear waste 62
Nucleus 26, 58, 59, 62, 64

**O**
Objective lens 74
Observed intensity 76
Orbit 10, 68, 69, 70
Ozone layer 18

**P**
Parallax 11, 75–76
Parsec 76
Peer review 5
Photon 16, 17
Photosynthesis 18, 19
Potential difference 30, 49, 50
Power 30, 32, 54
Pressure 80

# Index

Proton 58, 59
P-wave 7

**R**
Radiation 12, 16, 72
  background 59
  dangers of 61
  electromagnetic 16, 17, 81
  ionising 17, 58, 61
  poisoning 17
  protection 18
  uses of 61
Radioactive decay 59
Ray diagram 73
Real image 73
Red shift 12, 78
Reflection 7, 16, 21
Refraction 7, 72
Relative brightness 11
Renewable energy 27–28
Repulsion 48
Resistance 50, 52
Resultant force 41, 42
Retrograde motion 69
Right ascension 69

**S**
Sankey diagram 27
Sedimentary rock 4, 6
Seismograph 7
Sidereal day 68
Sievert 61
Signal
  analogue 20, 22
  digital 22, 23
Solar day 68
Solar system 10, 13
Speed of light 11
Speed–time graph 38

Star 12, 13, 68, 69, 73, 75, 76, 81, 82
  Cepheid variable 77, 78
  life cycle 83
  main sequence 82, 83
  neutron 82
  red giant 83
  structure of 81
Static electricity 48
Subduction 6
Supernova 82
S-wave 7

**T**
Tectonic plate 5, 6
Telescope 74, 84–85
Thermistor 49, 51
Transformer 26, 54
Transverse wave 7, 8

**U**
Uranium 63

**V**
Velocity 36, 37, 39, 41, 43
Velocity–time graph 39
Volcano 5
Voltage 26, 30, 51, 53, 54

**W**
Wavelength 8, 9, 72
Wave speed 9
Wind turbine 28, 29